See ya' at the airport!

The Colorful Stories of a Soaring
Contest Vagabond a.k.a. "The Gate"

By Charlie Spratt

See Ya' at the Airport!

Copyright © 2004 Charlie Spratt

First published 2004
Second edition 2011

Published by National Soaring Museum,
51 Soaring Hill Drive, Elmira, NY 14903-9204
assisted by BTLink Publishing

All rights reserved, including the right to reproduce this book or any part thereof, without the written permission of the National Soaring Museum

ISBN-13: 978-0-9763438-1-3

Cover design: Andrea M. Weissenbuehler
Illustrations: Greg Rosplock

Printed in the United States of America

I dedicate this book to Gren Seibels, who encouraged me to write. Without him this book would not have happened.

Publishers Note to 2nd Edition

This second edition of *See Ya' at the Airport!* by Charlie Spratt was updated to include a new foreword by Karl Striedieck, and two additional chapters: The Tube and Sailplane Racing News.

We thank Janice Hoke for assisting in the selection of news items for the SRN chapter.

Elmira, June 2011

CONTENTS

AUTHOR'S NOTE 1

- One -
KEEPER OF THE GATE 5

- Two -
MY PAL AL 13

- Three -
DEEP SIX 21

- Four -
RACE OF RACES 25

- Five -
WORKING THE LINE 37

- Six -
INFLUENCES: 53
Ben Greene; Gren Seibels; Dick & Angie Schreder; Johann Kuhn;
Klaus Holighaus

- Seven -
THE OH-OH SQUAD 63

- Eight -
THE CADET CLIPPER 65

- Nine -
HAULIN' GLASS: *The Grob Years* 69

- Ten -
HAULIN' GLASS: *Trailer Problems* 79

- Eleven -
GYPSY VILLAGE 87

- Twelve -
THE SIBERIAN EXPRESS... 93

- Thirteen -
GOOFY GATE.. 99

- Fourteen -
RHYME & REASON..107

- Fifteen -
THE JOKESTER..121

- Sixteen -
RULES ON THE ROAD 129

- Seventeen -
KIDNEY FAILURE 139

- Eighteen -
HALL OF FAME...145

- Nineteen -
THE TUBE... 153

- Twenty -
SAILPLANE RACING NEWS 157

SIDEBAR.. 187
Considerations for Charlie by Ed Byars
Kudos for Charlie by George Moffat

ACKNOWLEDGMENTS 191

INTRODUCTION

A theme that ran through Charlie's life was that he wasn't bothered by trivia whether in the realm of the physical world, interpersonal relations, or details that didn't seem to have an immediate impact. Readers will note this theme throughout the book and some of the conventional among us have reflected on how there might be a lesson here.

Another compelling aspect of Charlie was his uncanny ease with relationships, whether it be with a well-healed banker, professor, five-year-old, winner, loser, or average Joe. He was immediately comfortable with any and all, but wasn't fooled by the insincere or the pretentious. Therein lies another area for reflection as Charlie takes us along for a look at his life.

With this book, "The Gate" gives us everything from a bit of entertainment to a look at ourselves – both may be useful perspectives.

Karl Striedieck
Eagle Field, 2011

AUTHOR'S NOTE

I decided to write this book after a lifetime in the sport of soaring. I have been to over 200 sailplane meets in 36 years. The friends I have made over the years often suggested I write down the stories I was telling around the airport on rainy days. Sharing the experiences and stories from meet to meet made me the soaring gadfly.

The itch to travel came to me early in life. Like many teen-agers trying to find themselves, I went on trips and adventures anytime I could. Just as an example, a buddy and I took off for California one summer in an old van with very limited funds. We slept in sleeping bags on the floor of the van and found work when we needed cash. The feeling of freedom that trip gave me never left – I still get that old tingle every time I pack up and hit the highway on the way to another soaring adventure.

This does not mean I did not try to have a career. I decided that I would join the Navy and see the world. The thought of traveling the globe and getting paid for it had real appeal for me — I was a very naïve young man. I did see parts of Europe and South America, but

Author's Note

working on a salvage ship was hard dirty work and much of what I saw was through a porthole.

I came out of the Navy and went home to Charlotte N.C. I went to work for a "fixed base" operation on the municipal air- port, fueling all types of aircraft. It was at this time that I began a life-long attraction to aviation. I hopped rides with turkey haulers and bank check carriers. I learned a lot about what to do and not do in an airplane. I loved the work and being around the airport, but soon realized that if I was going to fly I needed a real occupation.

I traded in my fueler uniform for a coat and tie and went to work for my father's textile machine repair company. The money was better, but I had no time to travel or fly. I was living with a bunch of friends in huge houses around Charlotte. We had a friend whose father owned a real estate company that bought old houses to refurbish or tear down. He'd let us live in them until he was ready to change them. Then without notice, we'd be told it was time to move out. It wouldn't appeal to everyone, but it was an- other form of freedom I grew to love.

At age 28, after a couple of romantic disasters, my job was proving to be a dead end. The itch to dump it all and disappear got stronger, and I bolted for Florida with a buddy. It was on this trip that I made some decisions that have lasted to this day. The way it looked I was not heading toward marriage and kids. Without some driving force to make money I decided I'd try life without it. Rather than a goal, money became an inconvenience. I went after money when I needed it. I saved it until I had enough for the next adventure, then bailed out. From that time on I never had a job I wasn't planning to quit or a dollar I was not going to spend.

I discovered soaring in 1967 with some of my friends from the Charlotte Airport. We went down to Chester, South Carolina to fly a 2-22 one weekend and I met some folks in the sport. I began helping at soaring contests the next season at Chester. I loved the freedom of soaring. I started out working any contest job I could because it meant I'd be fed for free and allowed to sleep on the airport in my truck or van. The first summer I stayed on the road all season was 1973 — I went to seven meets that summer, hauling glider trailers for cash and working gates at the meets.

Since that time my focus has always been to get a few bucks

See Ya' at the Airport!

ahead in the winter and then hit the soaring circuit in the summer. This has lead to a wonderful life filled with bright summer days, millions of miles of travel, and an amazing number of real friends all over the country – and the world.

This book is about some of those adventures and people I have met along the way.

KEEPER OF THE GATE

I decided this story should go first, because it tells the tale of The Gate, where my place and reputation in soaring were established. It was written some years ago, when ground-controlled starts were universal, but the technology to replace them was already in view.

Blue sky, temperature rising. The last competitor rolls his sailplane into line, seconds before "grid time" is called. I radio the sniffer to launch as we all meander down to the middle of the grid for the pilots' meeting. There is tension in the air as I pass out the task sheets; the weather guru tells us that the lift will be great until the thunderstorms break. Meeting over, everyone settles down to wait for the sniffer's report.

Pilots and crews work quietly on all those last-minute details, preparing for the race, quickly downing a lunch of sandwiches and fruit with lots of liquid. The radio comes alive, the sniffer reporting *"I'm going through 2,500 feet AGL with two knots."* I announce over the radio that the contest launch will begin in fifteen minutes.

Keeper of the Gate

The next quarter-hour is spent talking with task advisors and pilots about the task and chances of getting it in before the sky explodes in thunderstorms. I cruise the line, stopping to talk with anyone who waves me down; we share the latest info and the latest joke circulating the ramp. Someone points to the horizon where we see the first cu of the day forming in the haze.

As time for the first launch approaches, tow-pilots start cranking their engines, slowly taxiing out of the tie-down area and rum bling alongside the runway to take their places in the launch line. "Ole Scratch," the head tow-pilot with thousands of tows under his belt, gives me a thumbs-up; I answer with thumb and forefinger formed into the universal "OK" sign. This silent connection gives me a feeling of confidence.

"CD, this is launch — we're ready to go." I answer: *"Start the launch."* Within seconds I hear the first tow-plane engine come up to speed and the race is underway.

After one more tour of the line, I drive my van over to the biggest motorhome on the airport, pull up and shout, "You guys ready to go?" I hear a muffled response and see some movement through the sun-shielded windows. Then the door bursts open and out pours the "gate gang." This is a loosely-organized group of young people, most in their early teens. They noisily pile into my van, sitting or lying anywhere they can, with at least two shouting, *"I've got shotgun, I've got shotgun."* Someone says, *"Here, Charlie, I fixed you lunch,"* as a sandwich hits the dashboard. In the back I hear, *"I have to go to the bathroom."* and then *"You always have to go to the bathroom!"* After I check to make sure all are aboard, and a stop at the nearest "Port-a-John," we head up a taxiway toward the spot that has been a huge part of my soaring life since I've been in the sport.

A picnic table, some portable chairs and a makeshift sun-shade straining in the wind are the features of this tiny spot on the vastness of the airport. It is "The Gate," and I have arrived with the team that brings this place to life. The kids leap out of the van, grab coolers and equipment needed to run the heart of the race. Chattering and giggling, they go about the business of setting up. The main radio is placed on the corner of the table with its mike lying in the chair under the strings that mark the start-line in the sky. The big binoculars are set on their tripod with their glass eyes aimed up; clipboards and watches are laid out on the table as each kid takes his place in this small but purposeful army.

During the launch, we sit in the shade, trying to get a wave from each competitor as he passes in front of us. My right-hand man, "Charlie Lite," shows up in his pickup and brings the latest from the grid: one pilot has had to pull out due to an unscheduled ballast-dump — the crew was working in the cockpit, accidentally hit the dump lever and couldn't figure out how to shut it off before it was too late. The gate kids are now in full-gossip mode while I look at my watch and the sky.

Cu's are forming all around the area and over on the mountains — the first sign that the weatherman was right. Above one of the cu's a large, white mushroom is growing into the sky. As the first calls comes from the IP, talking and giggling come to an abrupt stop. The radio operator takes her place under the strings as the spotter mans the binocs and begins his search for the sailplane approaching the start line. With one eye closed and a finger on the mike button, she calls "Mark," as the spotter announces the contest number. The timer writes down the number and time as the sequence person puts it at the top of her list. The spotter comes back into the shade; no one else seems to be at the IP.

Soon the conversation resumes: where they plan to go after the starts and who they can get to drive. Someone says, "Look out, here comes one!" We all see a dust devil swirling on the other side of the runway, headed our way. Clipboards are scattered, hands cover the open soda-pop cans and everyone bows his head, hoping the dust devil will not blast us too badly. It comes right into the tent and anything not tied down goes for a wild ride. "Grab my hat!" one of the kids shouts as it rolls and dances to the tune of the wind.

As a sailplane on tow passes in front of us the sequencer says, *"That's the last one."* The gate announces: *"Mark! The task will open in 15 minutes."* There's a pause while we figure out what time that will be: *"The task will open at 13:23."* Now more and more sailplanes are showing up at the IP, bumping up their start-time interval and running down the course line a ways to see how things are developing.

At this point the ragtag team suddenly transforms itself into a well-oiled machine. The radio operator is under the strings, the spotter is on the glasses and the timers are under the shade with pencils ready; all conversation has stopped. I check my watch and the sky again and wonder to myself, "What are these guys thinking? Can't they see those cu-nims on the mountains? Time is running out!"

The gate is clicking one start after another but all of us can see the gaggle forming down course. Already there are sailplanes drifting back from it for another run through the gate. Now the starts are at full force, with ship after ship hitting the mark. The window is working flawlessly as "good starts" and a few "bad tries" are announced. Truly, it is time to go — these starts are the ones that count. This team of young folks is up to the task, taking the heat without as much as a sigh.

"Mark!.. .Mark!... Mark!" the gate calls. Leaning forward, I say *"That's too close together — we need to separate them."* I get a look that says, *"Relax - we can handle it."* Overhead they are banging the gate at a rapid rate but no one seems overtasked, so I sit back and watch.

Now comes the quiet eye of the storm. Some have left on course, some are trying to play stealth-fighter as they jink and fly in different directions, planning to run the gate one more time for the classic "late start." The gate crew takes a short break, to the sound of pop cans opening and the rattle of snack bags. *"I bet Echo Mike starts last." "Nah, it'll be Whiskey Four." "Okay — you buy the Dairy Queen if Whiskey Four goes before Echo Mike." "You're on."*

Suddenly the radio comes to life with the first IP call of the last run — one more rush and it will be over. The spotter begins calling contest numbers seen at the IP; each gets a comment from the peanut gallery. *"I can't believe he's still here! What is he thinking?"* The spotter announces Juliet Delta is in the swarm; someone mentions this is the latest he's started since the contest began. Like a string of white pearls, they line up for the last start. This is the hot gaggle and as they move silently down the first leg we will watch the sky until they are out of sight.

Soon all is quiet again; the spotter can see no sailplanes in any direction. The team grows restless; the conversation is the hum of bored teenagers ready to be somewhere else. Checking my watch and the start sheet, I determine when they should return for the finishes.

See Ya' at the Airport!

"*Be back at 17:30,*" I say. "*What's that in real time?*" someone asks. I watch in relief and amazement as they gather their gear and begin the slow walk to the tiedowns. As they move on, the laughter and shouting drift away. Soon I am sitting alone under the shade with my thoughts about the day, the storms, the landouts sure to come — can anyone get around before the sky goes ballistic?

I call the window: "*Come on in.*" Charlie Lite arrives at the gate and we both start looking at the sky, wondering what direction the weather will take. I decide it's time for a little nap and move my van so I can get a breeze through the side door. I'm soon snoozing.

The sound of voices awakens me, I try to read my watch without my glasses and take a quick look at the sky. In the short time I've been out, the sky has exploded; off to the south I can see a dark column of rain hitting the ground.

I rejoin the gang in the shade; the conversation concerns the motel pool. Seems some rather large guest had dived into the pool and blown his swimsuit down to his ankles. "*I've never seen a moon under water... he had a lovely vertical smile.*" — teenagers are merciless to those outside their clique. I'm no better as I add my two-cents-worth to this mindless exchange.

For reasons that mystify me to this day, I have always been able to make contact with kids and teenagers. They treat me differently from any other adult. Many of my soaring friends tell me it's because I never grew up — maybe so, but I will always cherish these connections. For me, they are the sweetest part of the day — many times they have recharged my batteries and made a tough day a little easier. Since I have never been a parent, I don't have the responsibility of answering every question properly, and I do not have to react to certain words with horror.

Many times I have been asked questions I know they would not consider asking any other grownup. I always give them my best answer; not always the one their parents might give them, but always honest, with common sense and an understanding that they are moving through life at a speed seen only at this age. They are innocent, and that should be preserved as long as possible; but they also need to be armed with knowledge and understanding so they can enter adulthood with the weapons necessary to carry them to right decisions.

Keeper of the Gate

We sit at the gate waiting for that first *"Two minutes out"* call, but the sky is now overcast and muffled thunder is heard. I look down the last course leg and play the mind game: *"If they can get to that mountain or this cloud, then maybe we will see some finishers."*

Suddenly, like a camera's flash, lightning strikes a mile or two off the end of the runway, soon followed by the heavy crack of thunder. I order everyone into my van. The team hustles to get the equipment stowed and the radio under cover. I move the van again so the doors face the finish line, opening them so all can scan the sky.

Now the crew frequency is busy with messages short and to the point: Hook up and stand by — if you don't hear from me in five minutes, head out for Goat Ranch." "Alpha Zulu ground, go to the phones; I'm landing out — will call the lats and longs as soon as I get a chance."

Now I know this is a busted day but cannot help looking at my watch and continuing the *what if* game. The kids are talking about things that have nothing to do with the race; in a way it's a comfort to me, making me feel that this isn't a big deal and life continues on. I am distracted by their laughter and banter and soon join them in some "one-upmanship," only to be taken away by another land-out call.

Large rain drops begin to hit the ground; it is so dry, for a minute or two they stir up dust. All conversation stops with the first finisher's call: *"Four Zero two minutes out — what are conditions at the field?"* I instruct the Gate to tell him, *"Winds are west 10 to 15 with light rain."* The spotter is intently watching the horizon; the timers are checking their watches. *"I've got him!"* comes the shout, a finger pointing as we all squint to see. *"There!"* he points with a stabbing motion; someone else says, *"OK, I'm on him"* with the binocs at his eyes. *"It's Four Zero, all right, ballast smoking, fast as heat!"* comes the word from the backup spotter. I sigh with silent relief as he passes over and sets up on downwind to land. As I watch his landing closely to see what effect the winds will have, two more finishers call. Within ten minutes we have had eleven finishers, so I am feeling somewhat better about the task call and the day. The rain gives us a break, but obviously we're going to get a lot more, and soon.

Crews scramble to get tail-dollies and tow vehicles in place to avoid the rain. Soon the runway is clear; the chance of seeing more finishers is remote. I finally give word to the gang to head back to the tie-down area before the next squall hits. Someone's mom shows up in a van and they all pile in. Charlie Lite and I are left to wait until all are accounted for by the retrieve office.

In my nearly three decades of soaring I have spent countless days at The Gate: Classic days when the starts were hot and the finishes fast. Days when there seemed to be no end to the cu's as they stretched from horizon to horizon. I have seen days when it was so weak there were more land-backs than leavers. I have seen the drama of the race time and again, without tiring of its fascination. I had a front-row seat under those strings at The Gate. Best of all, I had those wonderful, bright, energetic kids to share it with.

Soaring has been my fountain of youth. It hasn't made me physically younger, but it has had a real effect on my heart and mind. I have sipped from this fountain so many times and have always come away renewed and refreshed. Those young people generate such power and energy (without any idea they're doing it); that makes the drink even sweeter.

I see these storm clouds on the horizon and I hear thunder. I know that this gate, this source of so much fun and input to my life will soon be a thing of the past. Technological progress will soon overrun it, as dark always overtakes light. I know that this is the twilight, the calm before the death, and I am saddened by it. It has been a great run; it gave me my place in the race; and introduced me to so many people and adventures that I have no desire to change any of it. Most of all, it showed me the best in those around me, and it gave me a family of children that would be the envy of anyone.

I know the day is coming when the scramble to get things set up, the nervous chatter before the start, the runs from the IP, the excitement of the finish will be just memories. Time marches on and technology replaces people; but the memories are mine and they will not be dimmed. My fountain may be gone, but its effect on my life will last until the end.

MY PAL AL

Like most of us I had lots of childhood friends but I was lucky enough to have one who was there from the start of kindergarten to long into my twenties. His name was Alan, but to me he was "My Pal Al." We had a lot of adventures together; this chapter describes a couple of them.

I grew up near Charlotte, North Carolina during the late 1940s and 50s. Little remains of the South I knew as a child. The summers were long and hot, filled with days of play imitating my heroes like Hopalong Cassidy and Roy Rogers. I can remember mornings of Cream of Wheat and biscuits followed by a few chores before being set completely free to roam the neighborhood. My mother would lock the screen door behind me with orders not to return until noon for my usual peanut butter sandwich and a glass of real milk. I know this is where the spark was struck that made my feet itch all those years after. The feeling of having nothing to do and the whole world to do it in has been a strong theme in my life ever since.

My Pal Al

Mostly, I spent time with Al — we were together every day. We played ball, met at lunch, and walked home from school together. We were a team in every adventure we came up with. As we got older some of this teamwork got us into trouble - what one would not do alone two could goad each other into. Soon we became famous around the neighborhood for our pranks and tricks. Some we did and some we did not do, but we got credit for anything that could not be pinned on anyone else.

By the time I turned 15, I think my mother just plain got tired of putting up with all our antics and us. With Al's mother in agreement it was decided that we would be exiled for a week to my family's small travel camper permanently based on a tiny rented lot some 15 miles from Charlotte on the Catawba River. Their plan was to drop us off with enough food for a day or so then return to check on us and re-supply the food. I am sure that in modern times this would not be an accepted plan, but the 1950s were a much more innocent time.

Typical of my mother, she had all the bedding and food we would ever need and after fluffing the dusty camper we were given "the rules." Al and I knew we were in an isolated place - it was some two miles up a rutted river dirt road just to get to the two-lane. From there it was another three miles to the nearest little settlement. The rules covered the usual things and included one very stern warning: my Dad's 15-foot Alumicraft fishing boat was *way* off limits.

The two moms got back in the Hudson and pretty much before the dust settled on the dirt road we were down on the pier figuring out how to get the boat unchained from the dock. Soon we are in the middle of the cove, pulling with all our might on the starter cord. The motor was a 30-horsepower Johnson and had a shut-off key. Al and I drifted back to the dock and began figuring out how to "hot wire" the engine. We got the connection apart with a pocketknife and within minutes we were zooming around the cove, laughing and plotting our next adventure.

The first thing we realized was that the boat was very low on gasoline. Checking all our pockets we came up with a little over a dollar. We took a risky chance that we could make it down the river to the only place on the river to buy gas. It was an old bait and snack store called "Joinners" at the North Carolina end of the "Buster Boyd

See Ya' at the Airport!

Bridge" the only bridge across the river in those days. We made it. Gas was 19 cents a gallon and we bought all we could.

We knew we were going to have to come up with a way to keep gas in the boat, but for now the freedom of buzzing from cove to creek was exhilarating. Al and I had occasionally picked up a few coins by scouting for and selling Coke and Pepsi bottles — you could get two cents a bottle and another dime if you had the crate they came in. We decided we could convert this business to the river with a little ingenuity.

The next morning we are on patrol and the pickin's are good. Lot of folks would lay out in the sun during the day and leave bottles on the docks and piers. Al and I would drift up to the dock and within seconds every bottle was in the boat. On occasions we would see crates stacked up behind a river house and with no one around they soon were on their way to Joinners for the deposit money. We were keeping gas in the boat and had enough for candy and Cokes as well. Life for two 15-year-old boys out on their own could not have been better.

Of course, we soon got a little bored with just running around in the boat. One morning as we come out of a cove into the main river Al sees a mud bar. With the thought of scaring me he heads straight for it. He misjudges the bar and before he can stop we are skimming over it. Unknown to us, the Johnson is not locked down so as we go over the mud bar the motor bounces up and we skid across, slick as a whistle.

Now it is my turn, and with the knowledge the boat will do it I'm at top speed. Both of us are howling with laughter and anticipation as the sound of the hull sliding over mud begins. Suddenly there is a huge jerk and we are now sliding sideways and slowing dramatically. We barely make it back into the water when Al shouts "Holy s**t." We both look in amazement at the back of the boat. Not only is the motor missing, the whole transom is ripped out of the back of the boat. We are dead in the water and sinking.

We jump out of the boat into ankle-deep river mud and try to follow the skid marks back to the engine. The stirred-up mud is making the search very tough. After some 30 minutes of struggling in the hot morning sun we decide we will come back when it is cooler.

Alumicraft was very proud that their boats were "unsinkable."

My Pal Al

They could make this claim because of the amount of white foam they put into every cavity of the hull. Al and I took turns towing the bowline as we started back to our camp. It was a mile by water but two miles by shoreline. We knew we had to be back by the afternoon as the moms were coming to check up on us and bring food.

We got back in time to rig the boat against the dock just as it looked before we got our hands on it. When the moms showed up we looked like two innocent teenagers who were bored but happy to be on the lake. The moms left feeling reassured that this exile was working and soon we would want to return home and become the good boys they knew we were.

As soon as they are gone we run back down to the dock to figure out our next move. With no transom and full of mud the boat is a sad sight. We are thinking of returning to the crash site for another search when Al comes up with what we both thought was a brilliant idea at the time. "Let's tell the folks that the boat got stolen!" I have no desire to hike back to the mud flat so I am taken by this idea. We talk and plot when it dawns on us that first and foremost we have to insure that the boat will disappear without a trace. We knew sinking it was impossible and trying to pull it far enough into the woods was impractical — we just weren't strong enough.

"We'll blow it up!" The idea came to both of us at the same time. Blowing it up would be a lot more fun, and easier. I must remind you that this is rural South Carolina in the late fifties: dynamite was used for stump removal; it was available in hardware stores and feed lots to anyone who had the money.

Al and I now had a ten-mile hike ahead of us, but the thought of the big explosion made the trek no big deal. We headed down that dusty river road with all our money in our pockets and heads full of how the big bang was going to solve all our problems.

We arrived at the combination saloon, bait, and hardware store — just walked in and said we needed some dynamite. "How big is the stump?" the young guy at the counter asked. Without blinking Al told him 15 feet. "Wow, that's a big tree — how'd you boys get one down that big?" "We just kept sawing," said Al. The guy tells us the price of one stick and after careful accounting Al and I figure we can get 8 sticks. He lays our purchase on the counter with a length of fuse. We

See Ya' at the Airport!

both realize we don't know one thing about setting off dynamite and ask for instructions. The guy demos how to set the fuse. Al says we'll need a minute to get away and the guy looks at him like he's crazy. "You're going to need to get a lot further away than that," he says. He cuts us 15 minutes of fuse and soon we are off with our dynamite.

Back at the camper there is nothing to do but wait for dark; seemed as if it took forever for the sun to finally go down and darkness to take over. We rigged the dynamite in the bow because it was the driest spot. Finally all is ready — we light the fuse and with a mighty shove send the crippled boat to the middle of the cove.

Fifteen minutes is an eternity when you are waiting for the big bang. We could see the sparks from the fuse in the dark as the boat drifted away from us. Standing on the dock we waited for the end to all our problems. I never heard the explosion. In fact, I don't remember anything until I came to. The first thing I realized was that I was no longer standing on the dock — I was embedded in the muddy bank some 15 feet from the dock. As I slowly came to I looked around and saw that Al was also embedded in the bank, 5 feet to my right. I called to him a couple of times but got no response. I have no idea how long we were out but I did notice a couple of sets of car headlights on the dirt road above the cove. This was unusual in rural South Carolina late on a weeknight. Suddenly Al lets out a shout and scrambles to his feet. He is stunned and from the look in his eyes does not know where he is. I notice a pretty bad cut on his left forearm. Both of us are covered in red river mud. We climb up the bank and head for the camper as a car comes to a screeching halt. Before the dust settles the driver is shouting something but both of us are having trouble hearing. Finally I make out his question: "Where did the meteor hit?!" Things went downhill from this point on.

Within minutes the local sheriff is on the scene. He takes one look at Al and me and knows no matter what has happened we are a part of it. He has one of those big spotlights on the patrol car and is moving it back and forth down around the dock when he sees something flash in the water. As he moves the beam out over the water the carnage comes into view. The boat is in three pieces now; none of it has sunk. Within a radius of 200 feet are enough dead fish to start a market. Most of the leaves on the trees near the bank are gone.

My Pal Al

We are put into the back of the patrol car and driven to the county jail in York, SC. Sometime around 4:00 am our parents are contacted and as the sun rose through the bars my dad appeared at the cell door. I just broke down and confessed the whole story. I would have gladly stayed in jail but the sheriff kept saying no real harm done and no charges were being brought.

The ride home was a silent torture. I expected the belt, but my sentence was much worse. There would be no more lazy summer days for me for a long time to come. My Dad owned a small textile machinery company and at age 15, I was put on a machinery gang working in the cotton mills in the area. Each morning at 6:00 I had to be ready to go and many days we worked until dark taking carding machines out of the mills for overhaul. I did that until school started in September.

I continued to have a fascination with dynamite but never did quite the damage I did that fateful night. I know both Al and I were very lucky.

Al and I went on to have many more adventures. As we got older cars and girls entered our realm and caused even more problems.

Both of us were excited by hot rodding, and as soon as we turned 16 both of us were busy building our "rods." Al had a 1950 Ford two-door with a flat-head V-8 that had three two-barrel carbs on top. I was running a 1951 Chevy with the "Big Six" and a four-barrel with custom headers. Those were exciting days and when I think back I realize we both are lucky to be here now.

The old camper at the river became our hide-out. Many summer evenings were spent racing down that old river road to see who could get there first. I would have a heart attack today if I drove like I did then.

Figuring out cars was easy for me — I have yet to figure out girls. All I can say is: I was trying real hard. One summer weekend Al and I decided to take our girlfriends out to the river for a day of swimming and sun bathing. By this time we had discovered the lure of beer on a hot summer day, and made sure the trunk of my Chevy was full of ice and cans of Pabst Blue Ribbon.

We spent the day lying out on the dock and jumping in the water when we got too hot. We made sure the girls got all the beer they wanted and by the time the sun was low on the horizon we all were feeling no pain. We went back up to the camper and, sticks sharpened, started roasting wieners over an open fire. Of course we are drinking another beer with every hot dog we eat.

Al and his girl drift off to the dock and I and my friend sit around the fire on a blanket. Remember this is the fifties — "going all the way" was a strict taboo. However "making out" was not and soon things are hot and heavy both on the dock and at the campfire. After another hour or so the girl I am with starts hinting that she has to go home to make curfew.

I wander down to the dock to get Al and his girlfriend and discover that Al, as usual, has drunk way too much. He is barely ambulatory as the girl and I help him walk back to the car. Al and his friend pile into the back seat where Al curls up and closes his eyes.

We drive back to town and I take the two girls to their homes; Al is totally oblivious to the whole operation. Now I must admit that in the past I had taken Al home, and in this condition I would drag him out of the car and lay him under the bushes that lined the front of his parents' house — when he sobered up enough to wake up he could climb into his bedroom window. The trick was to cut off the car lights and engine and coast into the driveway, then as quietly as possible open the door and get Al out.

Unfortunately, Al's mom had caught on to this trick and as I am getting Al out of the car his mother shows up beside it. The only thing she says to me is, "Get him inside." I am scared but put Al's arm around my shoulder and start for the house. Inside the front door I think the light sort of brought Al around. His mother is in her nightgown and robe with curlers in her hair and she is starting to rant when she sees his eyes are open.

The next 10 seconds went down as among the worst in parent-child relationship history. With his mom madder than I had ever seen her and Al so drunk that he did not know where he was, Al reached over and grabbed his mother. Al thinks that he is saying goodnight to his girl and with a "Honey I'll call you tomorrow", Al pulls his mother close and gives her a kiss. This was not a peck on the cheek — it was a full-blown French kiss!

Fear took complete control of me and without thinking I bolted for the car. I can remember saying over and over, "Goddamn I wouldn't done that," as I peeled a wheel in reverse getting out of that driveway.

The next day was Sunday and I dared not call. Monday morning I drive to school and park in the usual spot. Al's car is not there and as I walk in I see Al get out of his Dad's car on the school circle. I wait for him to get inside the building and, trying not to laugh, asked him how things were going at home. "What in the hell did I do?" It was not until I explained what had happened that he put 2 and 2 together. He lost his car for a month, had to do yard work every weekend, and was not allowed to associate with me. Shortly after this episode Al was sent off to military school. He did so poorly there that within 3 months he was back home and we were back up to our old tricks.

DEEP SIX

For some reason, this is my most-requested story. I actually got tired of telling it and decided it should be retired. But so many people have asked for it that I've included it here. I'm not sure if it belongs in a book about my life in soaring. You decide.

The late Fifties and early Sixties were a turbulent period for me. I sometimes feel that I learned everything useful in my life during the summer vacations from school. I loved cars and airplanes and never missed the chance to work on either one. I built "hot-rods," and the only impression I ever made at high school was when I accelerated my "open-piped, flat-head V-8" Ford out of the parking lot onto the open road.

This "lack of motivation" in school led to a suggestion by the principal that I should consider a career in the military. After some serious discussions with the school and my parents, the decision was made: On a cold, dreary day in January of 1962, I joined the Navy because they told me I could see the World. What they failed to mention was that the view would mostly be from a porthole, some miles from any shore.

I took to the life, and soon found myself on a salvage ship that traveled wherever anything had fallen into the ocean. We were on a "Med Cruise" in January 1966 when a B-52 bomber and a KC-135 tanker collided over the coast of Spain. Both aircraft were destroyed and the B-52's load of four hydrogen bombs fell to earth. Because the bombs were not armed, no nuclear explosions occurred; all but one fell on land and were easily recovered.

The missing one was a very serious problem with the Cold War politics of the time, not to mention that Spain was very upset to have a nuclear bomb near their shoreline. So my ship was dispatched at flank speed. Some 100 U.S. Navy ships were part of the operation, from battle cruisers all the way down to us. Our ship was the smallest, but because we were designed for salvage, it was up to us to do the grunt work of looking for the lone bomb that had landed in the water.

The bottom of the sea off Spain was like the land: rough and mountainous. The search was done with a TV camera mounted on a sled with controls much like an airplane. As the ship dragged the sled through the water the operator "flew" the sled along the bottom looking for the bomb.

We searched for more than two months before the bomb was finally found. We maneuvered into position and the sled with a special clamp bolted to its front made the first attempt to retrieve the bomb. Just as the clamp was closing on the bomb the sled moved and nudged the bomb down the side of the underwater mountain in a huge cloud of silt. It took another four days to relocate the bomb at a depth of nearly 3000'. After much careful work it was finally retrieved and brought aboard.

You could hear the sailors on the ships around us cheering as the bomb broke the surface. Like me, they were cheering because it meant that we could get some liberty after three months at sea. We came alongside one of the tenders and were relieved of the bomb. With thoughts of liberty and rest, we steamed away.

The Navy decided that since we had done such a great job we deserved the best liberty port in the Mediterranean. San Remo, Italy was the spot, and as we revved up the turns on the screw, all of us were reading about "Remo" and what it had to offer.

Finally we see land, and the order is given to prepare for docking. As we come into the harbor we see lots of people cheering and waving. Unknown to us, the newspapers have been carrying daily reports on the progress of this operation, and the local paper has made a big deal of the fact that the ship that recovered the bomb is coming to visit. We throw the lines over and as we winch in, the crowd grows and grows until they are all the way down the dock, and many are standing on the hill overlooking the harbor.

Our Captain was known for starting liberty early in his cabin with a drink or two, and when he saw all those people on the dock, something came over him. He decided the thing to do was put on a diving demonstration for these wonderful Italian folks.

This demonstration would show a hard-hat diver (known as a bubble-head) being put on a stage, lowered over the side, stepping off the stage, going to the bow of the ship, and jerking on a chain hung over the side — all to prove that we can actually breathe and walk under water (as I said, the skipper has had a few drinks).

At this point someone digs up the duty roster and finds out that I am the "duty diver," a mostly non-existent job, only required if the screw has been fouled, or on rare occasions when it needs inspection. I am sent aft to put on the 200-pound diving rig, which consists of a canvas and rubber suit and a heavy brass helmet. My shipmates are very anxious to get this over with so that we can start getting guys on shore and meeting some of the locals. *I'm* in a hurry, and *they're* in a hurry, so they load me quickly on the stage and I start down to the bottom for the demonstration.

The water alongside the dock is some 25 feet deep, and murky. I step off the stage and immediately sink into the muck and garbage that Italians have been throwing in this harbor for the past thousand years. Like all diving suits, this one has an air valve on the chest that will force "suit air" inside to make you more buoyant. I open the valve a crack and nothing happens. I open it wider — still nothing. I call on my intercom that I have no suit air and at that very moment someone opens the valve on the ship that they forgot in the rush. Suddenly I have suit air at 600 pounds of pressure going through that wide-open valve. Before I can react, the suit is completely inflated with so much

Deep Six

air that my hands and feet are fully extended, and no amount of trying is going to get my hand back on that valve.

Now my head is heavier than my body. Upside-down, I am quickly sucked out of the muck and headed for the surface. I break the surface like a bloated whale, helpless. In truth, this is a very dangerous situation as the air in the suit is trying to force my body into my helmet. I cannot breathe, and I can feel the pressure at my neck.

Of course the dive master understands my predicament, and in a second he jumps over the side of the ship and with his trusty bosun's knife he stabs the suit. The place where he stabbed the suit was not the best choice: right in the crotch. I am uninjured, but the air escaping the suit as I disappear below the waves gives the impression of the Pillsbury Dough Boy with a bad case of gas.

With the suit punctured I am now headed for the muck again, this time headfirst. I slowly sink into the darkness. I can now operate the valve, but it is useless with that huge hole in the suit. With great difficulty I manage to get a grip on the rip in the suit and by "burping" the suit I can pull myself out of the crud. I am still upside-down and do not have the strength to right myself. I began to add air to go up and release the rip to go down, hoping to find the stage and get on it. After some minutes I finally hear my helmet bang on metal, and with a final burp I land in a heap on the stage. In an exhausted voice I say, "Bring me up" and I feel the stage slowly moving.

I reach the surface completely spent, sprawled on the stage, with my embarrassing rip making some very strange sounds. I am finally back on board, with my shipmates literally rolling on the deck with laughter, and thousands of Italians cheering as they take my helmet off. The first words I hear are the Captain's, who says "No liberty for you Bozo, and I want that suit repaired before you go below."

I did finally get some liberty in Remo, and when I walked into the bar where all my buddies were they gave a loud cheer, and a salute, to the now famous Bozo the Diver.

RACE OF RACES:

The 1976 U.S. National 15-Meter Soaring Championships

American competition soaring has a colorful history filled with strong personalities, amazing advances in technology, and powerful politics. In 1976 the country was celebrating its bicentennial and competition soaring was on the verge of a new generation of sailplanes that would become the hottest racing class in the history of the sport.

When I first got interested in the sport, competition was "run what you brung." This was one-class racing no matter what your span or weight, and it was always exciting to see who could do "what with what." Those days were forever changed when the "Standard" class was formed. The original Standard Class called for no flaps and no retractable landing gear. The class was designed to limit competition to simple, relatively inexpensive gliders and separate the "big boys" from the "not-so-big boys." (Take a look at any modern Standard Class sailplane and you will see that those rules did not last.)

Race of Races

In 1973 Dick Schreder proposed another class to the IGC. At the time the difference between a flapped ship and a non-flapped ship was pretty noticeable. Dick proposed and campaigned for the "15-Meter Class." The politics were hot and heavy but Dick's idea was finally accepted: the class was designated official in 1976. Dick and Angie Schreder decided that they should stage the first 15-Meter contest at their home airport in Bryan, Ohio. They would promote it as much as possible to attract as many entries as the airport would hold.

Angie was the Contest Manager and she proved to be the very best choice. As a veteran crew, she knew who was right for each job. The first thing she did was make sure that Hal Lattimore would be the Competition Director. Hal agreed to leave Texas and come to Ohio to use his weather sense and task calling experience to make this the best contest yet. Neal Ridenour came on board as operations manager: he'd done several contests and was a proven master of the ramp. Jim and Jerry Rhine were the best gate operators in the country; they came from Oklahoma to run the starts and finishes.

I knew I had hit the big time when Angie asked me to oper-ate the start window. I was a true vagabond at the time: I traveled from contest to contest by hitching rides with pilots and crews; I slept in hangars and bathed in shop sinks. (I miss the lifestyle even now but just am not strong enough to live it.)

I arrived in style. I had met Ted Teach at a regional 1-26 meet in Maryland and he offered to take me to Bryan in his Bonanza. I thought I was big stuff as we taxied up to the big hangar – there were Ben Greene, Johnny Byrd, and Ed Byars standing outside watching us pull up.

Bryan is a one-runway airport with a line of T-hangars and one big hangar close to the road. Neal was really going to have his hands full getting 55 sailplanes into the air each day and then recovering them. The runway was 5,000' long, but it was narrow and the parallel taxiway was even skinnier. Some heavy power lines crossed the approach end of the runway. Dick owned the land around the airport and usually leased it out to a farmer. This year he had the farmer plant grass and this produced a great tie-down area.

I started scouting around for a place to stow my gear when Angie caught up with me and told me to use Dick's office. I checked it out and found a couch to sleep on and stow my gear behind. I was set to watch the great race.

Hal Lattimore, Jim and Jerry, and I had worked together at Hobbs in 1973 and '74 so there wasn't much gear-grinding as we all fluffed our nests. I have heard a lot of things said about Hal both good and bad but I will tell you now that he always treated the people who were helping him with a lot respect and humor. I was the window operator checking the height of gliders as they crossed the start line. The window was Hal's favorite place to be during the launch and the start. Over the years I worked with him we spent a lot of time out there and it was always entertaining.

Because the Schreders were such a large part of the Bryan community the local interest in the contest was more than ever before seen. The Bryan Times ran stories on pilots with lots of photos. The largest local radio station did live broadcasts from the pilots meeting and interviews with day winners. On many days spectators outnumbered the pilots and crews.

The rules for competition soaring were different in 1976. One of my favorite rigmaroles was takeoff time selection. Each day, each pilot chose his takeoff time, with the gate opening as soon as the first competitor left the ground. Pilots would listen to the weather report, contemplate the task, and somehow come up with a magic time to launch. Selection was done at the morning pilots meeting, and it rotated: the pilot who selected first today would be last tomorrow.

It was a show not to be missed. The best part was that after you picked a time you had the right to change it: you could not take another pilot's minute, but any open minute in the day could be yours. Usually the first pilot would name a time and the others would fall in behind him. This would continue until one of the contest leaders chose a time ahead of the growing pack. Suddenly pilots trying to be close to the leader would be piling onto the front. After this selection ended, the board – made up of hooks and buttons with four hours of time slots on it – would be moved to the front of the grid. Pilots were allowed to move their button with official approval.

As launch time approached, pilots would gather around to watch the board. I always loved it when someone like Ben Greene or Joe Emons would walk through the crowd, speak to the official guarding it, and casually move their button forward or back. As they walked away the crowd would scramble to change *their* times. This would often lead to chaos and soon Hal would be called to referee the game. One day the board was dropped by a young helper: I will never forget the terror in the eyes of that 10-year-old as buttons rolled down the taxiway in all directions.

In those days the task was set at the morning pilots meeting and it was always an assigned task. No task sheets were handed out; instead the task was on a blackboard that was kept covered until all administrative business and weather reports had been completed. I always enjoyed the moment when the task was revealed: a combination of groans and grumbling as pilots carefully copied the task information.

The first contest day was one of those "roll the dice" days. The weather report came by telephone from Detroit; Fred Keys was the weather guesser and he told the group that we were in for gusting winds and possible T-storms later in the afternoon. This meant the first guy to select would pick the earliest takeoff time allowed (12:30) and the rest of the fleet would stack up behind him.

As the launch got underway everyone was watching the dark clouds north of Bryan. Lift was around 2 knots with cloud bases at 3,500'. No one wanted to go out on course in these weak conditions, but the approaching weather was pushing them. The guys on the ground were wondering if they'd even get a chance to attempt the task. It was a shaky way to start the contest and as the day wore on many ships were scattered in fields on the second task leg to the north. But after a long quiet wait we were jolted to attention with the call "Sixty-two, one mile out." It was Laszlo Horvath in his 1-35, boring for the line.

Las was a very interesting person and pilot. His flying style was as flamboyant as his personality; on certain contest days he was unbeatable. (I was at his gliderport in Estrella, Arizona many years ago and he invited me to fly with him in a Grob Acro. After a couple of loops and a spin he asked me if I wanted to do an outside loop. To this day I'm sorry I said yes – it was the worst feeling I've ever experienced in the air. That's not to say Las did it wrong; in fact just the opposite – he was a very talented aerobatic pilot.)

The storms that cut the first day short were the edge of a front that killed any chance of a race on the second day. It was a great time for me to get to know some of the people I'd heard of but never met. All day the hangar was full of pilots and crews, and hangar flying was at its best. Best of all were the Schreder girls: Carol and Karen. They were veteran contest crews and they didn't waste time getting the fun started. They worked to get all the young people together and within hours we were talking as if we'd known each other for years. There wasn't much to do in Bryan, but these two knew where that little bit was. On many an afternoon we'd gather around the famous Schreder round swimming pool and plan the evening's entertainment.

The weather cleared by the next morning and Hal had a task on the board by 9:00 am. It was going to be a weak day as the ground was wet, but the wind had been blowing and things were drying out fast. Again there were lots of landouts but if you were willing to gamble and leave late, the drying created stronger thermals and higher bases. "Smokin'" Joe Emons won the day by flying 10 mph faster than Ben Green in second place. Joe was flying one of the most beautiful sailplanes ever built: the Scheumanized Libelle. For its time it was the ultimate: beautiful on the ground and fast in the air. Joe was flying it flawlessly and was at the top of his game in this race. (He's retired from soaring now, after more races than he and Shirley can probably count.)

Contest day three looked really good, and the task was the longest yet: a 180-miler west into Indiana. By now the ground crews were working without problems and Neal and his towpilots were flinging sailplanes into the air one a minute. It was impressive to watch eight towplanes handle launching and landing on one runway.

With Cu popping and lift in the 4- to 5-knot range with bases near 5,000', the gate was seeing its first real action of the contest. These were the days of the 3,300' start height, which meant lots of red-line dives. Jim and Jerry really had their hands full as ship after ship blasted through the gate. I was on the strings and the pressure to see each sailplane as it called in was intense. There were several "bad tries" as lift would fill the gate during a dive, making it impossible to hit the mark. I always hated to call "bad try" because I knew how important a good start was. Because of the low start height, the first thermal on course could be the most important part of a contest flight.

Race of Races

The recovery operation could get tight if we had lots of finishes in a short period. Fred Pakosta got squeezed into making a "go long" landing on the side of the runway, and could not quite avoid running into the VASI light. From the gate we watched Fred get out of the ship, walk around to the dinged wing and rub the leading edge. He then walked over to the VASI and gave it a kick. That must have hurt, because the next thing we saw was Fred with a bear hug around the VASI, wrestling it off its stand and throwing it to the ground. Later, Fred reported that the VASI had suffered some damage during his landing that he'd be glad to pay for.

Jim Smiley was the winner that day with a speed of 51 mph. That might sound slow compared to the speeds flown today, but the low start height combined with the performance and limited weight of the gliders made this a pretty fast day. Jim was the kind of racing pilot who played his cards close to the vest: his "winner's speeches" were famous for revealing nothing about what he had actually done to win. (Jim drifted away from competition soaring and stayed gone a long time. He's now back, and has admitted to me that things have really changed.)

Hal Lattimore caused another rumble at the next morning pilots meeting by announcing a 200-mile task. It covered three states with turnpoints at Adrian, Michigan and Goshen, Indiana – a classic two-turn assigned task. Lift in the 6-knot range to above 5,000' led to plenty of "start-gate roulette." It was a great racing day with Joe Emons being the first guy to double up as a day win-ner.

This was the 4th of July and the holiday, combined with good publicity, brought a large crowd of locals to the airport to see what was going on. It was really amazing to overhear spectators talking about the pilots and where they stood in the race. (On several days, pilots who landed out were surprised that the farmer knew who they were and where they were supposed to be going.)

For a national race, the gate and window had to be perfect. Jerry and I spent several hours working with a towplane to insure that the height of the "window" was right on. The window was made up of two tall pipes about 20 feet apart with the main string strung tight between them. Ropes and stakes made sure it stayed rock-solid throughout the contest.

See Ya' at the Airport!

With the crowd on the airport it was impossible for the window not to be noticed and arouse curiosity. Sure enough, during the hottest part of the start a local shows up, and in walking toward us, stumbles over one of the stakes and falls into the lines supporting the contraption. With the fall and flailing, the window is knocked completely out of whack. The guy gets up and asks "What in the hell is this thing for?" Hal shows no emotion as he answers, "It's a bird trap – we are trying to catch the southern Ohio redneck stumble-thighed goonie." The guy had a good comeback: "I think you just caught one." We all had a good laugh and in a few moments the window was back in business.

The fifth contest day was another "pucker maker." As the launch started, rain could be seen off to the east. If you were lucky enough to be at the front of the grid you got launched into lift; toward the back things weren't so good. By the time the last few were ready to go, rain was on the field. Off tow it was a long run to the sun, a quick climb and then a trip back through the rain for a start attempt. Several pilots landed at Bryan and never got away. Joe Emons started early and won his third contest day. After the race the Schreders put on a big barbeque for the contest, and the locals finished off by a huge fireworks display at the town square.

One entertainment for the kids was Jim and Connie Indrebo's dog "Ratso." Ratso was a small black dog of unknown lineage who loved nothing more than chasing a Frisbee. But he was so small that he couldn't get his mouth on the disc unless it landed upside-down. If it didn't, Ratso had no choice but to push it with his nose until it hit a bump or pebble and flipped over. He'd then grab the edge and drag it back to anyone who would toss it again. It was so funny to watch him push that Frisbee around, sometimes for minutes at a stretch. The game finally had to end: Ratso bloodied his nose and paws pushing that Frisbee.

Next morning's weather report is not encouraging. A high dewpoint and a forecast of T-storms tell everyone this is a day to get going early. The first available launch time is moved up to noon and the pilots just say "next" as the takeoff selection list is called. As the guys are going through the gate, Cu are already towering. By the middle of the afternoon pilots are flying through rain, thunder and

Race of Races

lightning as they try to complete the short 116-mile task. Dark clouds form over the airport as crews gather near the retrieve office.

One by one, contest numbers appear on the landout board. Just when we think no one will get home, Pete Newgard drifts over the finish line. This brightens the faces of crews who have not heard from their pilots; several get back in their cars and head for the runway. Sure enough, finishers are showing up with just enough energy to get through the gate. Several cannot make the gate and must try to roll across the line. As the last few arrive, a light drizzle covers the field. Soon it is a downpour.

Then, out of the rain and mist comes Bobby Bridges in his PIK-20. Bobby is slow and low and the rain is playing havoc with his glide. Bobby lines up on the runway, flies *under* the power lines, and flops onto the pavement. His problems are not over – the rules say you must cross the finish line. Bobby rolls and rolls through the rain; finally his wingtip goes down less than 100' short of the line.

Larry Rogers, also flying a PIK, made a safe landing in a very muddy field. The farmer saw him, grabbed a raincoat, and slogged into the field to greet him. When Larry opened the canopy the farmer asked him why he landed in the field. Larry gave the guy the usual story about lift, sink and weather; when he was finished, all the farmer said was, "Well, the airport across the road there has a paved runway."

Johnny "Birdman" Byrd won the day. Johnny is considered by his peers to be the best cloud reader in American soaring. His ability to follow cloud streets and find the hottest spots is legendary. Johnny won this difficult day at a speed of 55 mph – 7 mph faster than the second-place finisher. (Johnny and Ann Byrd are retired now and living in a home they built overlooking the high desert near Ft. Davis, Texas – not far from the famous soaring site of Marfa.)

The Bryan Soaring Club put on a little impromptu potluck dinner in the main hangar and all of us hung around most of the evening to hear the land-out stories. When all are known to be down and safe these evenings can be very entertaining and are a real part of the sport.

At the pilots' meeting for the seventh contest day, the forecast again calls for T-storms. We launch early on a 130-miler, hoping to get in a task before things blow up. Everyone is on course when Hal Lattimore comes on 123.3 to warn pilots and crews that a strong storm

See Ya' at the Airport!

threatens Bryan with hail and high winds. The field comes alive with crews hurrying to tie down trailers and secure loose gear. The storm comes close but its main force falls west of Bryan.

With one bullet dodged, what could be next? The radio tells the story: We begin to hear pilots reporting zero visibility and strong turbulence on course; it sounds like all are cut off from returning to Bryan. It's decision time. Some decide to try to run around the storm to the north. But the storm spreads out faster than they can run and they all land out far from home.

Others find good lift away from the storm and decide to hang out, hoping it will move. Four early starters are out ahead of the main fleet: John Byrd, Brian Utley, Burt Meyer, and a young Sam Zimmerman are caught under the storm but see breaks in the clouds toward Bryan. Byrd and Zimmerman strike out for home, thread the needle and make the finish line. Utley, a thousand feet below them, lands 2 miles short.

I will never forget Burt's finish. The storm is raging just west of the airport with scruffy clouds all the way to the ground. Suddenly, out of this turmoil breaks an HP-11, flying dead level and heading for the line. Burt crosses the line and lands safely. Later he tells me it was the roughest flight of his soaring career.

We had one more miracle to go. After the storm finally died and all thoughts of anyone finishing were gone, a 1-35 flew silently across the finish line. A huge cheer came from the tiedown area: in the days before air retrieves were allowed we all knew this was a real finisher. It was Bernie Carris – he waited out the storm for over two hours.

The winner for the day was Sam Zimmerman. Sam was really coming into his own at this time. Having flown several regional contests in Chester, South Carolina, he was ready for the big time and this day proved it. (Sam and Leigh are still seen at many contests, and Sam is still a threat to win any task he flies.)

The forecast for day eight was the same: more storms with lighting and thunder. Hal Lattimore called another short task in hopes of getting them all back in the box before the skies opened up. There was no "start gate roulette" – by now everyone knew what was coming. They had a good run for most of the task and most were back in the box by the time the rain hit. The few who gambled with a late start gave all of us on the field a real show with low, slow finishes over the trees: the last useable lift was some 15 miles from Bryan.

Jim Smiley was the fastest, but had a problem. We were using cameras, and turnpoint pictures were subjective to say the least. The only time you could be sure of no argument about a photo was when the film was blank or the pilot took the picture from the wrong end of the runway. Jim did the latter.

This put one of my all-time soaring heroes into first for the day. Ben Greene had taken me under his wing when I first started working contests at Chester. Ben was the classic southern gentleman and the way he talked about soaring let you know he truly loved the sport. We all felt for Ben at this race because of his back: Ben was injured landing a fighter on a carrier deck during the war in the Pacific. Long flights in a glider would aggravate the injury and on several days Ben needed help getting out of the plane and would then have to lie in the grass a few moments. (This injury is what finally took Ben out of the sport: after an operation to relieve the pain, Ben found he did not have the ability to operate the rudder like he felt he should be able to.)

Finally the weather that had plagued us for the last three days was predicted to blow out with an approaching front. After an evening of beers and hot dogs followed by a long-into-the-night party, I headed for my trusty couch. I was awakened about 2 am as the front rumbled and thundered overhead. I can remember thinking that this would mean great weather for the final race day. Suddenly a flash of lightning lit up the office, followed instantly by a *loud* clap of thunder. As I rolled over thinking it would soon pass, I felt something heavy land on the couch and start burrowing alongside me. I leaped up, thinking the Tasmanian Devil had finally found me. It turned out to be the Schreders' dog "Thumper" who was deathly afraid of thunder. From the looks of the screen door, Thumper had come through it near the speed of sound. Thumper and I had become friends during the contest, but not as close as he wanted to be during this storm. I sat up with him until the thunder was a distant muffled sound, then showed him the door. Next morning at the pilots meeting he came in and lay down beside me with eyes staring as though to say "Thanks."

Hal Lattimore lived up to his reputation on the last contest day. Many thought he would be conservative with the final task call after the pounding the pilots had taken during several stormy days. But

See Ya' at the Airport!

when the task board was turned over the distance was 211 miles – the longest of the contest. It was another classic triangle with the first turn at Warsaw, Indiana then a long run up north to Marshall, Michigan. The leaders chose middle and late starting times showing they had confidence in the weather briefing, which called for a good long soaring day.

Throughout the contest the towpilots had been warned repeatedly to stay high over the power lines at the approach end of the runway. These lines supplied power to a plastic plant down the road. All had gone well until now. Mahlon Weir (subject of another chapter in this book) was the tow pilot who caught the wires on the last tow of the last day of the contest. The rope wrapped around the main line and almost brought Mahlon's Maule to a midair stop before the wires broke. It was early afternoon and according to the owner of the plant every mold in the place had plastic in it when the lights went out. The heaters that kept the plastic fluid were lost. The workers at the plant spent the next two days scraping the molds clean, and rumor has it that SSA insurance paid the bill.

The runs through the gate were a little less intense as it became obvious that no storms were going to spoil this day. It was a long and lazy wait around the pool as we listened to the few and brief calls from pilots to their crews. A little after 5 pm, Dick Schreder steamed over the finish line in his beautiful HP-18. All pilots got home, the last one crossing the finish line near 7:30 pm. Woody Woodward won the day (not an uncommon feat for Woody). Joe Emons won the contest with John Byrd right behind him.

We held our last "ramp cadets" party that evening. It was a fun time with some sadness mixed in. We'd wave madly as crews and trailers drove out of the airport. We talked about the next contest we planned to attend and how we hoped all our new friends would be able to be there also.

There is nothing more quiet or lonely than an airport the day after a big contest. Trailers gone, tents and sunshades pulled up and stowed and no roar of towplanes all add to the forlorn feeling. But I knew in my heart that I was now hooked on competition soaring. I have been a part of it ever since this race.

WORKING THE LINE

There are few jobs in life that you enjoy day in and day out. Early on in my search, I was lucky enough to find work that was fun and never boring – working at an airport. This chapter presents just a few stories from that phase of my life.

My first airport job was working at a fixed-base operation on the municipal airport in Charlotte, North Carolina. It was in the late sixties and Charlotte was not yet a big city — more like a wannabe. It was growing, but still had the old-time Southern flavor that so many of us now miss. I worked the line, fueling aircraft from huge jets to single-engine bug-smashers — I saw them all and appreciated every one for what it was. It was roustabout work, full of machinery of all types. Being part of a fueling crew there was always a chance for a practical joke, or some ribbing to be mixed with the work.

The most interesting part of the job was the people that came through the doors of the big hangar and into the office. The rich, the famous, and the unknowns all had one thing in common: the love of flying and its use in everyday living. I met Charles Lindbergh on this job and spent an afternoon with Roy Rogers. I was given a $100 tip by Arthur Godfrey, and shook hands with Johnny Carson. I saw governors, senators, preachers, and hustlers of all types. All on the same ramp, I saw real aviators and people who could not taxi, much less fly. It was a wonderful exposure to flying, and imprinted me with a feeling for flying and flying people that I've never lost.

Haskell Deaton

Haskell was a short, round man who always wore a tweed jacket and a nondescript tie. At some time in the dim past Haskell had flown airplanes, but no one could remember when, and his stories of his aviation exploits were the fodder for back-room jokes around the airport. Haskell was a bookkeeper for a small, family-owned motel out on the strip that paralleled the main runway. He mostly worked as the night desk manager, but never mentioned it — in conversation, he was always "the accountant." Haskell for the most part was a quiet man in his late forties, living in one of the motel rooms. He had one problem and that was drink. He didn't do it constantly, but it was a habit, and when he drank he became a different man. As his nose got redder his personality got bolder, and he would embark on a night of adventure in the local taverns and bars, telling of his vast flying experiences.

On occasion Haskell would meet a lady. According to how many drinks she'd had and how dim the lights were, Haskell could actually cast the bait and get a bite from time to time. He'd tell her of his harrowing flights across Africa, or about his gold mine in Argentina, or maybe his story of the millions he had made in Alaska filing mining claims and selling them to prospectors. As the evening went on and the drinks crossed the table, the time came to really sink the hook. Haskell would invite the lady to fly with him to Miami for a champagne breakfast, and a couple of days at his villa on the beach. He always portrayed himself as being from out of town so he would stand up and announce that he was going to call a limo, unless of course she had some other mode of transportation. It worked every time, and they would pile into her car and head for the airport.

I worked the night shift at this time, and knew I was in for some fun when Haskell showed up. He'd get out of the car, walk around to

See Ya' at the Airport!

the driver's door and help a very unsteady woman to her feet and toward the office. As his friend would go to the restroom, Haskell would come to the desk, slip me a fiver and, acting as if he didn't know me, announce in a loud voice, "Young man, please get my plane out of the hangar and prepare it for a flight to Miami." I would slip the money in my pocket and say "Yes, sir, Mr. Deaton."

I'd then go to the hangar, hook the tug to whichever of the large corporate planes was closest to the front, and tow it out of the hangar and under the lights. With the keys off the board, I'd unlock the plane and turn on the interior lights. Soon Haskell and his lady would wander out, with Haskell telling her all about the engines or the latest radios he'd had installed. As they climbed in I would say, "Will there be anything else, Mr. Deaton?" "Perhaps a little refreshment, young man. Is she topped off?" "Yes, sir, she's ready to go." "Thanks — I'll be back in about a week." As I left the plane, the look on every one of these ladies was the same: through red eyes I could see them saying, "I've caught a big one this time!"

In a few minutes I'd return with a bucket of ice, a couple of glasses and a bottle of Seven-Up. Haskell would thank me and turn to his guest: "Why don't we have one more for the road?" They'd go up into the cockpit and with drinks in hand, Haskell telling her even more about his adventures in this very plane. Soon the drinks were drunk and the moment of truth was at hand. Haskell would get out a Sectional and fake some knowledge about night flying. Just at the right moment he would turn to his new friend and say "I'd better go check the weather. You sit here and finish your drink while I make sure we have clear sailing down the coast to Miami."

Haskell would stagger out of the plane and into the office. He'd give me the sign and I'd turn on the loudspeaker in the hangar that was used to make public announcements; the microphone was right beside the telephone. Haskell would dial some numbers. "Is this the weather station? Fine, I need to know what the weather is like between here and Miami." With his finger holding down the microphone button, Haskell would carry on a conversation about fronts, clouds and anything else that he thought would make him sound like he knew what he was doing. Before long, we'd hear: "HURRICANE??? Oh my goodness, when? Yes, I understand. You think it will hit first thing in the morning? This is bad news — I'm trying to get to Miami tonight. Well thanks — we'll hold off for a while."

He'd return to the cockpit, and acting as if he didn't know the loudspeaker was on, tell her that there was a hurricane headed for Miami and it would be very dangerous to fly tonight. He'd refill their glasses as they sat and thought. Suddenly, Haskell would come up with a great idea: "Honey, I know a small motel right close to the airport. Why don't we get a room, get some rest and tomorrow we can make the flight — the hurricane should be gone by then."

This ploy worked every time, and as Haskell drove off toward the motel and I moved the plane back into the hangar I must admit I admired him a little bit. For here was a short, round little man who was drunk and was going to score in a world where that doesn't happen too often.

Curtis Turner

Charlotte is the home town of NASCAR. Curtis Turner was a NASCAR driver famous in the early days of this very popular sport. He was known for his hell-bent driving style and for his even more hell-bent lifestyle.

Curtis flew a twin-engine Aero Commander. It was tied down on the far corner of the tarmac and as far as I could tell never saw any maintenance. Curtis had a habit of showing up on the ramp, leaving his car in the middle of everything and hopping into the Commander. With no preparation, he'd hit the switches and start taxiing as soon as one engine lit off. Many times he would arrive at the runway still cranking the other engine and take off as soon as it was running. He never taxied to the end of the runway – he always pulled out right where the ramp met the runway.

I was working the night the first "hijacking" took place in the US: some passengers on a flight from Miami decided they wanted to go to Cuba. This act put the whole country on notice: for the first time airports were trying to establish some kind of security. At the Charlotte airport the order came down: all access gates must be closed and locked. Now the truth was that many of these gates had not been closed in years. Along with several other "ramp doctors" (called that

See Ya' at the Airport!

because of our white uniforms) I spent hours cutting down small trees and clearing dirt and weeds to get the gates closed.

Curtis flew in that night. As the Commander rolls to a stop he jumps out and heads for his car (a brand new Rolls-Royce). I am fueling a plane at the stationary pumps as he drives by. Within a minute he's back: "Charlie, why in hell are the gates closed?" I tell him about the hijacking. "Well, who can open them?" I tell him the orders came from the tower.

Curtis is always in a hurry, but he gets out of the car and goes into the office to call the tower. After a few minutes he comes storming out, cussing and shouting. "Stupid – no one up there knows anything!" He gets back into his new Rolls and drives toward another gate: locked. He tries two others and finds them locked as well.

Suddenly I hear tires squealing and the engine revving as Curtis takes things in his own hands and charges the main gate. Still accelerating, the heavy car hits the gate and explodes through it. Into the dark goes Curtis without his headlights, headed for town. Scattered along the road are the gate itself and several very expensive car parts.

On another occasion I was dozing at the FBO desk when I heard the unmistakable rumble of Curtis's Commander rolling onto the ramp. I look at the clock and it is a little after 3 in the morning. I expect Curtis to walk in but he does not appear and I figure he has gone home without the usual stop-by. I'm back to dozing when suddenly the door bursts open and Curtis staggers in. He has obviously been drinking, but that is not the real shocker: he does not have on one stitch of clothes.

In a mumble he says he wants to go to the Sleeping Bear Motel, about a mile from the airport. I go into the hangar and find an old warming blanket used to cover engines in winter. I get Curtis to wrap up in the blanket before I drive him to the motel. Curtis is well known at the motel and when we arrive and wake up the desk keeper he soon has a room. I drive back to the airport and settle back in for some more snoozing. I did notice that the Commander was parked at the in-ground fueling station, but I decide to wait until morning before putting it back on its tiedown.

I'm back at the desk with my feet up, near sleep, when I hear a small voice calling, "Curtis, where are you?" I open my eyes and see the face of a woman peering through the door. "Have you seen Curtis?" She is standing beside the door with just her head in view. As I walk toward the door, she says, "Don't come any closer – I can't find my clothes!" I become aware of this and tell her to go to the ladies room while I try to find her clothes.

I go out to the Commander and even in the dark I can tell that there are several other people without any clothes. They are sacked out throughout the aircraft. Back to the hangar for more blankets: I toss one into the ladies room and take the others out to the plane. Soon I have three women and one guy standing in the office with nothing but blankets on. I load them all into the van and we head for the Sleeping Bear. Not one word is spoken on the trip. At the motel all are given a room to crash in.

A week later I saw Curtis. All he said to me was that it was one hell of a party.

The Runaway Luscombe

One Sunday afternoon I was working the gas pumps. The ramp was filled with weekend flyers and the pumps were busy. My job was to wave in any transient aircraft that taxied by. With the fuel hoses stowed in the ground, fueling was easy if you got the guy to taxi right up to the spot. I had three colored cards in my pocket. As a plane taxied up I would hold up a card guessing what grade of gasoline the plane used: red was 80 octane, green was 100, and purple was 140. When I got thumbs up I would direct the aircraft to the correct pump.

I held up the red card as an all-aluminum Luscombe taxied up. I'd never seen this plane before but it was in beautiful shape: the aluminum was highly polished and the chrome prop flashed in the sunlight. The pilot gave me thumbs up and I got him to the right spot for 80-octane gas. As he shut down I grabbed the ladder, but the pilot quickly informed me that he would do the fueling – seemed he didn't trust "lineboys" to fuel his beautiful plane without dragging the hose over the wing. I opened the pit, set the meter and handed him the nozzle.

While the pilot carefully fuels I take a quick tour around the little beauty. It has a perfect interior – it's obvious someone has spent a lot of time getting it just right. No hangar rash or dents and even the belly is spotless. I ask the guy how it got it so shiny and he matter-of-factly tells me he polished it with baking soda and baby powder. "That's a lot of rubbing," I say and for the first time get a little smile out of him.

He finishes gassing her up and carefully hands the hose back to me. I ask if he would like for me to prop it, as I know it has no starter. He declines, telling me he has a perfect system for starting the plane by himself: He reaches into the cockpit and sets a small "matchstick" behind the throttle knob. He then goes out and pulls the prop through a few times. A quick return to the cockpit to switch on the ignition and he is ready to start the engine.

I don't know if he forgot to remove the matchstick or accidentally moved the throttle knob. But after a couple of pulls the engine starts with a roar. In an instant the Luscombe is taxiing without a pilot.

The pilot panics and tries to get into the cockpit as the plane is speeding across the ramp. But it's moving so fast that his attempts to get the door open and the throttle pushed in are fruitless. It's all he can do just to hold on.

Down the ramp and onto a taxiway goes the Luscombe – the guy is steering the plane by dragging his feet as he hangs on the strut. He can only turn the plane to the left. He steers the plane off the taxiway and down a runway. All of us on the ramp watch in awe as this guy goes down runways and up taxiways, trying from time to time to get into the small cockpit but without success.

I get an idea from my days of flying U-control gas model airplanes. In the hangar is a pile of old blankets. I grab a couple and draft one of the other guys on the ramp who has a pickup truck. He manages to get the truck in front of the Luscombe and I make my first attempt to stop the engine by throwing a blanket into the prop. The attempt fails – the blanket is shredded. We line up again and this time it works – the blanket stalls the engine and the Luscombe at last rolls to a stop.

The pilot was ecstatic that his desperate struggle ended with no damage to the plane. The same could not be said for him. Dragging his feet had destroyed his shoes, and the tops of his feet were bloody. We called an ambulance. As he left for the hospital, we pushed the plane back to our hangar.

A week or so later the pilot showed up at the airport on crutches.

He was happy to see his plane and seemed even happier to see us. Later that month I came to work and noticed the Luscombe had departed. A week later a check came in the mail for me and the guy who drove the pickup truck. It was a great way to end a very dangerous situation.

The Ercoupe

During the summer of '72, I worked for Bermuda High Soaring at Chester, South Carolina. I kept the tow record each day, answered the phone and did any job necessary to keep the operation going.

One busy morning, in the middle of getting all the planes ready, the phone rang. The guy at the other end was very enthusiastic about soaring, and wanted to tell me all about it. I did the usual "uh-huh" act, trying to be patient. At last he got to the point: he was planning to fly up the next day from his home in Florida to take lessons and add a soaring rating to his license. I told him we would be waiting.

Not only was I working in the office, I was sleeping in it. Each night I got a folding bunk out of the back closet and set it up. An airport is a very lonely and quiet place when all are gone. The next day was a busy one, with tows and students from 9 am to 9 pm, but by 11 I had my bed ready and soon was snoozing. Naturally, I'd completely forgotten about yesterday's phone call.

Sometime after midnight there is a loud banging at the door. I am startled awake and shout, "Who the hell is it?" thinking one of my buddies is playing a joke. The guy gives his name but I don't recognize it. "I called yesterday telling you I would be here today!" I stagger to the door and unlock it.

He's a lot more awake than I am: he's talking a mile a minute, but it's hard to say exactly what about. Now fully awake, I realize he is describing a landing he has made — not on this airport. He landed near dark — he could not find the huge Chester airport from the air. He spent the last several hours hitchhiking and walking to get here.

He tells me his plane is in Lockhart, South Carolina. My first thought is that there's no airport in or around Lockhart. He explains that he flew around for more than an hour looking for the Chester airport and finally, very low on fuel, decided to land in the biggest clear spot he could see. He wants me to drive him back to his plane so he can take off and get it to Chester. We agree that early morning would be a better time for this, and I find him a place to curl up in the corner of the hangar.

Next morning we're up before dawn and ready to go. I should have known something wasn't exactly right when, in addition to a gas can, he asks for a broom handle, some duct tape and a hacksaw.

The place he chose to land turns out to be the front lawn of the old Lockhart Cotton Mill. This mill was built back in the mid-1800s and was originally powered by a water wheel. We drive up just before dawn. The front lawn is surrounded by a chain link fence about 6 feet high and is clear except for one small tree near the sidewalk that leads to the office. Though the mill shut down some time ago, the lawn is well maintained. But it's short - less than 200 yards between fences. Near the front door of the mill sits an Ercoupe - a 65-horsepower, twin-finned airplane famous for the fact that it can't be spun and is flown like driving a car.

What happened during the landing is now evident: the guy hit the single tree with the left wing, leaving a divot in the leading edge. Without hesitation he climbs the fence and asks me to pass him the repair kit. He does a rough measurement and with the hacksaw cuts a section of broom handle. With this wedged in the leading edge and covered with duct tape he has repaired the damage. I back the truck up to the fence and from the bed hand him the gas can. He pours it all into the little plane and, just as the sun breaks the horizon, he cranks up and taxies down to the end of the lawn.

With all 65 horses wound up, the guy starts his takeoff run.

Very quickly it becomes obvious that there is no way this operation is going to succeed. I am expecting a shutdown that never comes. At the last possible moment he yanks back the yoke in a desperate attempt to make the plane hop the fence.

Believe it or not the plane clears the fence; the problem is the landing gear. Both wheels are below the top of the fence and what was barely flying is not in an instant. The plane hits on the other side of the fence with a terrible thump. The instant silence is stunning. I am running toward the hulk when a black car passes me; on its side I see: "For official use only." As I come near I can see the guy standing beside the totally destroyed plane. He has a cut on his forehead but other than that appears OK. Next I see a couple of guys in suits and ties getting out of the black car.

It seems that someone noticed the Ercoupe in the mill yard and called the local sheriff, who in turn called the FAA. The FAA guys arrived just in time to see the crash first-hand. They assumed I was just a passer-by, so I was totally ignored. Within minutes they had the guy in the back of the car and sped off. I looked at my watch: a little past 6 am. I headed back for Chester with a great story to tell.

That afternoon the pilot called to say we could have the plane if we'd move it. We all went down to Lockhart and loaded the wreck on a Schweizer trailer. It was a total loss: we saved the engine; the rest was buried on the Chester airport. Later we discovered the engine case was cracked, so it was heaved also.

I have no idea what the FAA said or did to this guy, but we never saw him again. He left his home in Florida to learn how to soar, but he never did any soaring and he lost his Ercoupe.

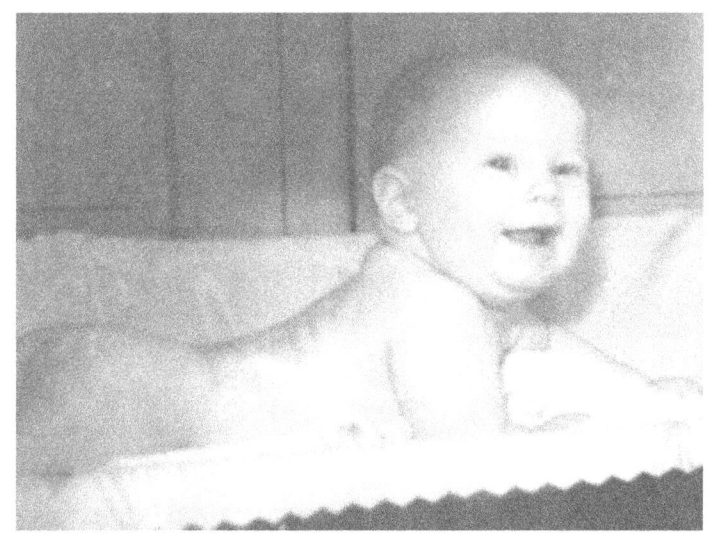

Charles Augustus Spratt, born in Charlotte, North Carolina on February 25, 1943.

Mary Choice Spratt holding her son Charlie while visiting Dad at the base inDayton, Ohio, early 1944.

Charlie about 8 years old.

Normal Park Elementary School, 4th grade. Charlie thought his teacher, Mrs. Will Holt, was the most beautiful woman he'd ever seen. Charlie top row, 4th from left.

'My Pal Al' Alan Aitken, Charlie's childhood friend and partner in crime, around 1972.

USS Petrol, ASR (Submarine Rescue) going into Malta, 1964.

Charlie with inflated diving suit that he wore during his "Bozo the Diver" adventure.

Charlie watching the gate, Ionia, 1983.

Painting the shed used for the gate crew at Uvalde, Texas in preparation of the World Championship, 1991.

On the scale in Mifflin, Pennsylvania when challenged by pilots and crew to lose weight during the contest. Charlie cheated and won.

Charlie wearing a glider t-shirt.

With Connie Bowen, Ann Byrd and Bo & Leigh Zimmerman around 1978.

INFLUENCES

I was lucky to get into sailplane racing before the end of the "golden era." It was a time of amazing advances in sailplanes and the way they were raced. The men who flew in the late '60s and early '70s were creating modern soaring. Because the sport was new to me and I was becoming part of it, those whom I met remain large in my memory. Many have now slipped off the score sheet, but the things they did are still with me. As I became more immersed in the sport it became evident to me that I was dealing with the best class of people I had ever met. In this chapter, I'd like to describe some of them.

Ben Greene

Ever the Southern gentleman, Ben Greene is just such a pilot. I met him on a soaring weekend in Chester, South Carolina. In the late '60s, on the weekends, the challenge was always a cross-country. Ben and several others had just run the famous Monroe-Pageland task. Like always they had raced from the last turn to home and there was a lot of jousting and joking as the planes were tied down. As the sun was getting low and with all the flying done we would sit around the trailer and hear the blow-by-blow of the flight. It was on these weekends that I realized the kind of people that are in soaring. Ben was the first to include me in this group, and his mentoring steered me through the early days of finding my place in racing.

Ben not only flew sailplanes well, he had flown fighters in the Pacific. I spent several evenings asking Ben about his military flying. It was hard to get a whole lot out of him but I did learn that he had flown Hellcats in combat against Japan.

We were at a contest in the early '70s in Adrian, Michigan. With poor weather, a group of pilots and crew decided to go to the movies, Ben and I among them. The movie was "Midway" and the theater had the latest in sound systems: "Surround Sound". We settled in with popcorn and cokes to see the hard-nosed Americans take on the Empire. At last the great battle began. Suddenly, as though a rock-and-roll-crazed teenager had got his fingers on the volume control, the sound went to the max. We were literally holding our hands over our ears as the bombs, machine guns and screaming planes came on the screen. After a couple of minutes Ben leaned over to me and shouted, "Charlie, I was *at* Midway, and believe me it was not this loud." We both laughed until the last explosion.

Ben suffered from a back injury caused by a hard landing on a carrier. He was tortured by this for years, and finally had to go under the knife to relieve the pain. The operation stole soaring from him by reducing his ability to react quickly with his feet. He had no choice but to retire from the sport he loved. Even this was done with a grace seldom seen. Ben was a huge influence on me in those early times; he set the standard by which I judge myself in any racing situation. On very rare occasions he will appear at a race. The second I see him my mind flashes back to those wonderful days and all he meant to racing.

Gren Seibels

Gren Seibels was another who influenced me greatly in the beginning. Several years ago someone called Gren to ask if he knew me and was I good enough to work a start gate. Gren's answer was typical of him, sharp and to the point. "Do I know Charlie Spratt? Hell, I *invented* him." That is the truth. When I first began to work

See Ya' at the Airport!

the start gate in contests the system left a lot to be desired. The ships would cross the start line in silence. Only after the gate crew was sure that a sailplane had started would they call on the radio and announce "good start." This system was not very friendly to the pilots, and occasionally pilots would complete the task only to be told they never had a good start. This caused great friction between pilots and officials. I came to Gren with an idea to say "stand by" as the sailplane approached the gate, and then "MARK, good start" as they crossed the line. In the sixties this was radical thinking, especially coming from a young vagabond with bushy hair and wearing sandals.

Gren, in his usual style, thought for a moment then said "Try it — anything is better than this goddamn system we've got now." It was at this moment that I was invented. With these few words coming over the radio the pilots knew when they were close to the line, and hearing their call sign followed by "good start" meant they could head out on course knowing all they did would go on the score sheet. It was from this one decision by Gren that I was able to build a thirty-year adventure that has taken me around the world, and established my place in racing.

For Gren, soaring was a large portion he took from the table of life. Gren once said that for any endeavor to be worthwhile it had to have three elements: one, "it has to be difficult enough to be daunting;" two, "it has to be irrationally expensive;" and three, "above all it must be useless!" By that he meant that it must have no pragmatic value, no profit potential.

Gren saw soaring as an escape from the ordinary, a chance to search the soul. "While racing a sailplane, it is impossible to brood over taxes or business aggravations or in-laws. To compete with any hope of success requires ferocious concentration, along with a deep-seated faith in one's indestructibility." And, "If soaring is useless, so is painting, wine, poetry or great music. Without such enhancements, our lives would be diminished, drab and barren." Soaring was like a wine to Gren, and he flew with a joy seldom seen.

Gren was a former television newsperson. His command of the English language was noteworthy, and his ability to use it could make you feel warm and fuzzy, or cut you like a knife. Not only did he and his wife Trudy organize the races in Chester, they also raced in them.

Influences

In the midst of trying to get the contest underway a crew from Gren's old TV station showed up to film the race. Seeing Gren on the ramp they immediately approached with lots of questions and demands. Gren knew launch time was close, but agreed to a brief interview. With the film crew standing everywhere in the way and a rather aggressive young woman shoving the microphone in his face the filming began. Gren slid into the cockpit, with the young lady asking a hundred questions a minute. "What's this?" and "what's that?" were ringing in his ears as he tried to get ready for a long task. Finally, in order to get it over with he began to show and demonstrate the various controls in the cockpit. "This is the flap lever, as you can see they go up and down. This stick controls the ailerons that bank the plane, and also moves the elevator up and down. These pedals control the rudder, and this knob releases the towrope. "What's this lever?" the woman asked, pointing to the landing gear handle. Without thinking Gren grabbed the lever and before he could say, "This is the landing gear" he pulled a little hard. KABANG! was heard all the way back down the grid as the Libelle collapsed on its belly, and Gren momentarily lost his control of proper English. Needless to say, this piece of film did not make the six o'clock news. Those of us left on the ground after the launch gathered around the camera crew. Time after time as each was allowed to watch through the camera viewer Gren was seen to drop like the condemned on the gallows, and a laugh was heard every time his startled face turned to the camera.

Several years ago Gren made the hardest decision a pilot has to make - to quit soaring. I am sure it was the right one, but I must admit it took some of the light out of the start of the season not seeing him and Trudy on the ramp. Because of his faith in me I was now in demand at other racing sites. Soon I was traveling the country running gates. It was the beginning of a wonderful adventure.

Dick & Angie Schreder

I really began to travel from contest to contest in the mid-'70s. I was in Hobbs in '74 for the first contest held there, and I was lucky enough to be invited to Bryan, Ohio in 1976 for the first

15-Meter contest ever held. I had met Dick Schreder a couple of times but never had a chance to know him. All this was to change at

See Ya' at the Airport!

Bryan. Dick has done things in racing that will never be done again. Designing, building, and winning Nationals with his famous sailplanes made Dick one of a kind. Watching him show up at a contest with the sailplane still in production, working all night before the first contest day, then going on task and winning was very impressive. Not only was he a winner at contests, he produced kits of these wonderful ships for others to build. He was the champion of the "low-ballers," and the father of the 15-Meter class. Over 400 of his kits were built, and many are still flying today.

The contest at Bryan was a great success, and the 15-Meter class was well established as the new class to race. Over the two weeks of the race Dick and I became friends. When the race was over I was invited to travel with the Schreders to Hutchinson, Kansas as crew. On the trip out I discovered the secret of Dick's strength: Angie. She was a person with insight, and a high-caliber mind. We talked for hours at the table in the motorhome, as Dick drove. We covered many subjects but the one most important to me was Soaring. Angie knew who the movers and shakers were, and she had an opinion on all of them. She gave me an overview of the racing scene that I used many times, and her instincts were all right. To this day I consider Angie the one who opened the door for me in racing. I know Angie spoke well of me among the other crews, and this led to an acceptance that made things much easier for me.

Angie came to many gates over the years to help with the timekeeping, and spotting. Those long afternoons waiting for the pilots to return were spent reading and talking and our friendship grew stronger and stronger.

We were working the gate at Chester together one afternoon during the finishes. Dick flew through the gate with several others and set up to land on the main runway. The gate was located to give us all a fine view of the landings. As Dick arrived on final we noticed that his gear was not down. I called on the radio "'1' - check your gear." I repeated the message with more urgency as he got closer to the runway, with no results. Dick was some ten feet off the ground as he passed the gate. All of us were waving and pointing frantically as he floated by, to no avail. He landed in a shower of sparks and with a terrible noise. Now Dick was known for never drinking coffee or whiskey, and never saying a curse word. On this landing he was able to keep two of his virtues intact. Angie and I were instructed to get under each wing and raise the ship so the gear could be extended. On our hands and knees we strained and strained but could not get the ship high enough to allow the wheel to be lowered. Dick finally said, "This has never been so hard before." Angie took a deep breath and relaxed for a second then said "Dick, you're right, but the last time we did this you were OUT of the cockpit!" With that remark we all began to laugh, and it was several minutes before we could get it together to get the gear down and the glider off the runway.

Both Dick and Angie were very powerful positive influences on me. Dick passed away on August 2, 2002, and Angie is no longer part of the racing scene. But I will never forget the friendship they have shown me.

Johann Kuhn
I was working the gate at Chester during the annual "Mini Nationals" in the spring of '78. This was before the rules restricted the number of entrants, and we had the same number of pilots as the year, 78. It was a good day, and the gate was really "poppin." Pilots were making diving runs to bump up their start time interval, as other classes were starting on their tasks. Even in this busy time there are moments when nothing is happening. During one of these breaks I was getting a swig of water, and putting on more sun screen when I noticed a guy leaning on the hood of my old truck. We spoke and I noticed a German accent. "How's it going" he asked. With my usual youthful swagger I replied, "It's cookin', but I can handle it." Just then the radio cracked with yet another racer at the IP, and I returned to the job at hand.

After an hour and a half of heavy gate it was over, and the timers were comparing sheets to make sure everyone was accounted for. I noticed that the guy was still there and struck up a conversation. He asked several very pointed questions, and very quickly I realized this guy knew a lot about sailplane racing. Finally, I looked him in the eye and shook his hand and introduced myself. He gave me a strong grip, and said "Johann Kuhn." At the time I did not know who he was, but I was soon to find out. After several minutes of conversation Johann asked, "Is there a possibility you can come to Ionia, Michigan for the regional this August." I never turned down such an offer, and immediately say "YES."

This meeting with Johann was the real beginning of my education in the art of competition directing. Ionia is a beautiful racing site in the heart of Michigan. Because it is between two of the Great Lakes the weather can change on a whim. The ability to get a race day out of what appeared to be nothing was Johann's specialty. Many days we would sit on the runway with gray skies above and grumpy pilots all around. Just when you thought he was crazy the sun would suddenly brighten the ground, and soon the sound of towplanes cranking filled the air. Many of those tasks were short, but the test was equal for all. Over the years of racing I have noticed that pilots often remember the weak and scratchy days, and how they saved themselves better than the great days when they finished somewhere in the pack. I have been to many contests where the Competition Director called off the day only to see later that we could have flown. With Johann this never happened. That lesson has paid off more times than I can remember over the years.

Another lesson Johann taught me was how to handle pilots who think they have been wronged. There is nothing worse than having a red-faced pilot in your face telling you that he is going to protest or worse. Johann had the perfect solution. He would say in his calmest voice, "Let's meet in one hour in the scoring office, and sit down and talk this over." Then with a friendly smile he would turn and walk away. What this did was give the pilot time to cool down, and give Johann time to do some investigation. This system worked every time, and he avoided the worst trap in competition directing: face-to-face shouting matches.

We were in the midst of a Nationals in the early '80's and the weather had been tough. The ground was so wet that we could not grid in the usual grass alongside the main runway. The runway at Ionia is plenty long, but typically not very wide. The dance it took to keep all the cars and sailplanes on the hard stand was a practice in patience. Just as we were all lined up ready for launch the wind decided to do a 180 and blow from the North. The wind gained speed quickly, and it became obvious we could not launch 60 sailplanes full of ballast

Influences

downwind. Johann had a habit of speaking in German when things weren't going right. (One time I asked his daughter what he was saying. She looked at me with a quizzical stare, and said, "Can't you tell cursing when you hear it?") His decision was the only logical one given the circumstances: the first shall be last today.

The elephant walk began with everyone having to hand push the ships to the other end. Johann was standing at the gate on the hill above the runway watching the procession, and speaking in German. Out of the chaos came three pilots walking up the hill. One was a multi national champion, one the leader of the race, and the third a known troublemaker. They told Johann that what he had done was against the rules and they planned to protest. He listened politely, but stuck with his decision - every day that can be flown in a nationals should be flown. When the pilots left the hill Johann really began to abuse the German language. Between bouts of shouting he told me that if these fellows didn't fly and filed a protest that the day would be a total waste. The launch began and from the heights the first few reached it began to look like a better day than predicted. We were sitting at the gate picnic table watching the sky and the launch when the tug flew by with the multi national champion in tow. Johann looked at me with great relief on his face and said, "Ah, the children go out to play." He was so happy that we did not hear any German for the rest of the day, and he treated the whole gate gang to ice cream after the starts.

Johann taught me a lot about racing, and how to avoid many of the traps CDs can fall into. Not only was he a great director, he was a great craftsman. Johann was a modeler for the automotive industry in the period when all new cars were modeled in clay before production. He had wonderful hands, and could turn a total sailplane wreck into a pristine restoration. He always had a project of some kind going, and loved the work. Johann was a strong family man, and they supported him fully at all the contests. In every phase of the ground operation there was someone related to him working. Hilda not only helped Johann, she took on the task of doing the annual contest pig roast. Never in all of soaring have I eaten such well-prepared food. I'm convinced that many came to the contest to eat the pig roast and the soaring be damned.

See Ya' at the Airport!

I last saw Johann at a convention in Chicago. His illness had ravaged him and he was weak, but in his eyes was the same spark I had come to know. When he spoke of his problem he would talk quietly in English followed by some of that German in much stronger tones. I seldom get the chance to return to Ionia, but occasionally I do, and when I see that big white hangar and the little clubhouse on the side I am always reminded of the man who taught me so much about this amazing sport.

Klaus Holighaus

In the late 1980s I was in the middle of a political storm mostly having to do with where I was going in competition soaring. I was doing a lot of contests each summer, not only working the start gates but also as Competition Director. Much of the "old guard" in the sport felt that I did not have what it takes to be a CD. I had been a CD in many Regionals, but every time it came up that I should do a National contest it would not happen. Once at a site in Georgia I was scheduled to be the CD, but when I arrived on the airport I was quickly told that someone else would be doing the job – someone who'd never before been CD at any contest.

I was working the gate at Uvalde in August of '88. Klaus Holighaus had come from Germany to fly the now-famous Texas thermals. I'd never met him but of course knew who he was. On the afternoon of the third contest day this thin small man with a thick accent showed up at the gate. Many pilots had finished and more were on the way. Klaus stood under the gate shade and watched with interest as sailplane after sailplane crossed the line. When things calmed down he came over to me and started talking. He told me that the way I got the guys through the start gate was the best system he'd ever experienced — letting the gate flow freely gave the pilots a real opportunity to choose the start time they wanted. He explained that in Germany they only let one sailplane at a time go down the "slot" and get a start. This clogged up the start and many pilots could not start right when they wanted to. Klaus was very interested in taking this system back to Germany and even invited me to come over and show the system to his club.

We continued to talk and I explained that I was having real

Influences

political problems over some of the things I was doing. He gave me some great advice: "Ignore what you hear and never take the bait they are throwing — if you continue to do for soaring what you have done here you will prevail." He was very enthusiastic in this statement and as the contest went on we became better friends.

Klaus was a very positive influence right when I needed it and because of his advice I did prevail: in 1990 I was a national CD for the first time. I sent Klaus a postcard telling him I had broken through the political barrier. A few days later I got a phone call at a regional in Dansville, New York — Klaus had taken the time to find out where I was and call me. His congratulations meant a great deal to me.

THE OH-OH SQUAD

All sports must have an Oh –Oh squad that forms when some event demands it. It seems to be self-generating and anyone can become a member. Soaring seems to have more than its share of them. I think this is due to the complex nature of the sport and the fact that it is an endeavor and not a profession.

For many years a sailplane meet was held in south Georgia, and it became known as the "Cordele Ordeal" — anyone who is going to be outside in late August in Georgia is in for a hot ordeal. The combination of humidity, heat, and gnats can make the most timid of personalities turn into a cranky, short-tempered, cool-seeking grump.

The trick in Cordele was to get up early, get out to the airport and assemble your sailplane before the sun got much over the tree line. This cuts down on the sweat factor, and kept you cool and calm for the race.

Not all are aware of this veteran trick, especially pilots new to the sport. While the "old hands" are back at the motel, sitting in their rooms with the air conditioning turned on full, the new recruit is on the ramp with his bride trying to wipe the sweat from his brow while lifting wings and taping gaps.

Coming to the airport in time for the pilots meeting with the idea of assembling afterward sometimes can be a rush. In haste to get to the grid on time, one pilot discovered that he did not have his Sectional chart. "Honey, you forgot to bring my Sectional from the motel," he shouts. His wife makes some remark that she is not responsible for this part of the equipment, but dutifully jumps into the Land Rover, cranks up, and drives off. Everyone hears the "crack" of fiberglass as the Rover heads for the airport gate: in her rush to leave she has managed to run over the last foot of the wing. To make things worse she doesn't realize she has committed this crime — she is driving away with the windows up and her hand in front of the air conditioning vent waiting for that wonderful burst of cool air.

Within seconds the Oh-Oh squad forms. They examine the injured wing while every few seconds one of the members says "Oh-oh, look at that" or "Oh-oh, this looks bad." The squad grows larger, and soon the "Oh-ohs" are coming fast and furious. Suddenly one of the members looks up as the Rover comes through the gate and says *"Oh-Oh."* All members look up and in unison say *"Oh-Oh!"* which is the signal for the flock to disperse.

This squad can form anytime, anywhere. I have seen it around the scoring shack after a racing day. One of the more famous moments begins when pilots gather around talking with the winner of the day. They talk about thermals: "Did you catch that one just out of the second turn?" "No, but I saw it – you guys were really climbing." "I got over ten knots for two minutes in that one," someone pipes up. "I had trouble coming out of the fourth turn," says another. The face of the winner turns pale. It seems in the heat of the race he forgot that the task was changed in the air, and that there were four turns instead of three. "Oh-Oh" is muttered by everyone standing around as the "former day winner" quickly goes back to the score sheet and sees that fourth turn, big-gerthan life, printed in black ink at the top of the sheet. The squad is very sympathetic while in the flock, but as they turn to leave you can see a smile on each face, and the giggles among them as they walk away.

THE CADET CLIPPER

During a contest day, a gliderport is a busy place: gliders overhead, the roar of towplanes and the radio chatter make for an exciting time. At night it is the opposite: the ramp is quiet but the kids at the contest, trapped at a remote airfield with a pilot who went to bed early, are still full of energy. Over the years they and I have come up with many forms of entertainment to while away the evening hours. This is the story of one of those adventures.

For many years I have been a part of a rag-tag bunch known as the Ramp Cadets. This army is made up of "crew types" and "ground-pounders" who don't fly in competition but are dedicated to sailplane racing. Ramp Cadets come in all shapes and ages with just one restriction: no competition pilots. The reason for this rule would be obvious if you were ever in a group of racing pilots: all they talk about is racing. For those of us ready for something else after a hard day of crewing, this is very boring.

Hobbs, New Mexico, is one soaring site that loses its appeal the minute you step out of the crew vehicle into that blast-furnace wind

The Cadet Clipper

and realize there is no shade within two miles. Heat, dust, and Vinegaroons (the largest and ugliest bug I've ever seen) do not add charm to this racing site. While the racing pilots are frolicking in the 70-degree stratosphere, cool and comfortable, those of us doomed to the ground feel like we're melting into the asphalt.

But while Hobbs can be bad during the day, it can be just as good in the evenings. Soon after the sun goes down, the place turns into a tropical paradise. The temperature drops into the pleasant 70s, a southerly breeze comes up and the moon and stars are at their brightest. You could pay a couple of hundred dollars a night in some exotic vacation paradise and not get the feeling of that cool breeze. That breeze, and the fact that there are no bloodsucking bugs, has led me never to sleep indoors at Hobbs.

These pleasant nights invariably give the Ramp Cadets a second wind and suddenly these sweat-soaked, dust-blasted kids are looking for some action. Now, let's face it, the entertainment industry in Hobbs leaves a lot to be desired, and most of the older soaring types are long into their motel rooms by 9 p.m., leaving the Cadets on their own. Like a magnet the ramp draws them back to the airfield, and the word spreads: "RAMP PARTY TONIGHT!"

At the beginning of the race I was issued an old Nash Rambler station wagon by the contest manager, Jack Gomez. This was for moving people and equipment around the airport during the contest. The Rambler was tired, and years in the desert had taken a toll on its paint. There was no license tag, so the old car couldn't leave the airport. I discovered that at idle the Rambler would cruise at about seven mph; since it was an automatic I was soon having great fun turning the steering wheel hard to the left or right and jumping out of the car, leaving it doing donuts. I would carry on business while the old station wagon ran in circles, much to the delight of all who witnessed my "daredevil" stunt.

During a rather routine ramp party an idea struck me that was to change Ramp Cadet history. I sent scavengers to find some old tow rope. Within minutes we began to change that old Rambler into the *Cadet Clipper*. With a half-filled bottle of warm beer we christened our new "ship" and made preparations to get underway.

I sat on the roof, my feet over the windshield. With the towrope

See Ya' at the Airport!

tied to the steering wheel and led through the windows, I was ready to put to sea. The other sailors piled onto the hood and the top and with a flick of the shift lever into drive, we were underway. I soon discovered that sailing was even greater fun with the headlights off. We charted our course by the light of the stars. Out in that ocean of concrete the chances of running aground were nil, as long as we stayed in the sea lanes (runways). The old car radio had no antenna; the only radio station it would pick up carried country and western, period. To the sounds of Hank Williams Jr. and Willie Nelson, plus the giggles and rap of teenagers, we set sail on the "Sea of Hobbs".

Not all was smooth sailing. Unknown to us, the Hobbs police had been having trouble with people coming on the airfield at night to drag-race and shoot guns. The police were carrying on an active campaign to close the field at 10 p.m.; anyone found there after curfew was in serious trouble. As we were navigating the main channel, headlights appeared at both ends and began to approach us at a high rate of speed. By the time I was able to get down off the top and into the driver's seat to stop the *Clipper*, blue lights were flashing and several Cadets had blinding flashlights in their faces. After several minutes of intense interrogation, with our names written in one of the officer's books, we were allowed to return to the ramp with the warning not to drive on the runways ever again.

Sailing on the *Cadet Clipper* had quickly become the best thing to do after hours. After the next morning's pilots' meeting I was asked at least twenty times, "Will we sail tonight?" I didn't say yes or no, but after the start gate closed, I took the *Clipper* out on the runways by myself to see if there was some way we could have our fun and stay out of trouble. As I drove I realized that we didn't need to stay on the runways: the whole place is flat as a board and there was nothing dangerous about being off the pavement – just some scrub brush and sand. Sure, we will sail tonight – and any other night we feel like it!

All pilots accounted for, the gate closed, and the ramp dark and deserted, the *Clipper* quietly slipped out "to sea." Lookouts were posted to keep a sharp eye out for the dreaded "Coast Guard." We had been at sea for a short time when, as we rounded the far taxiway, headlights were spotted on the horizon; the sound of large V-8's was unmistakable.

The Cadet Clipper

We hear the engines' deep roar, as one set of lights heads off to port, and the other heads straight for us. I turn to starboard and we wander out into uncharted waters. I warn the crew to keep quiet and cover everything that could throw a reflection. Fear and near panic grip my young crew as the lights close in, but just as we are sure we have been spotted, the "cruiser" passes 200 yards astern. Fear turns to joy when we realize that we have escaped detection! The cruisers regroup off in the distance. Side by side with their lights on bright, it is obvious they are planning another sweep. I bring the *Clipper* about and start sailing directly toward our adversaries. In a moment of true foolhardiness, I send my first mate below and on my signal she turns on our headlights. Instantly, we hear the screech of tires, and four very bright lights are headed straight for us. Quickly, I shout, "turn 'em off" and tack to port, out into the black unknown. We watch in amazement as again we are missed – the confusion of our enemy is obvious. Now the cruisers start a search that consists of roaring up and down runways and taxiways in no order. I am worried that the cheers of my crew might give us away.

The time to escape is at hand. I scan the horizon for a landmark, and spot the old ammo dump with its high mounds silhouetted in the dim light. If we can make those mounds we will never be found on this dark night. The course to our haven crosses several "sea lanes," but with careful navigation and several zigzag patterns we arrive at our safe harbor. The crew scrambles ashore and up to the top of one of the mounds. From this vantage point we watch as the cruisers continue their search. Soon, things quiet down and we reboard the *Clipper*. We head for the home port with the crew reliving every moment of our victory at sea and already planning tomorrow night's sortie.

I have worked many contests at Hobbs since the *Clipper* last set sail. After a day of racing when the ramp is dark and quiet I can almost hear the waves crashing ashore, and see the mast passing slowly, with the laughter of the crew faint in the air. Not a racing season goes by when one of that crew doesn't send me a postcard or letter reminding me of the fun we had. Little do they realize that it was I who was having the most fun: the kind of fun you never forget, sailing on the Sea of Hobbs.

HAULIN' GLASS: *The Grob Years*

For some twenty-five years I towed glider trailers for a living. It took me to every corner of the country, and showed me adventures almost too numerous to remember. Just a few of these are the subject of the next two chapters.

For the most part towing was a routine business made up of Interstate miles and truckstop food. Cheap motels and limited TV were the evening's entertainment. For long stretches the only people I spoke to were motel clerks and waitresses. I was never bored because there was always someone to see along the route, and some place to explore I'd never been before. I loved the life and miss it terribly.

I hauled every kind of glider trailer you can imagine from the latest model with a new ship inside coming off the docks to homebuilts clabbered up from pressboard and a 1949 Ford rear axle with the original tires. I drove pickup trucks and later vans. I never paid more than a few hundred dollars for them and spent lots of time making them tow-worthy. I took pride in getting 3 and 4 hundred

Haulin' Glass: The Grob Years

thousand miles out of them before finally selling them, many times for more than I paid. In the millions of miles I've towed I've had most every kind of mechanical disaster known. Broken timing chains, U-joint explosions, water pump failures, and blowouts have brought me to a sudden stop many times. Each time I fixed the problem myself and with dirty hands and filthy clothes drove on feeling the satisfaction of total independence. In all those years of towing I never so much as dinged a trailer, or damaged a sailplane. I chalk it up to lots of luck and lots of checking everything all the time.

That's not to say I didn't come close to disaster a few times. Back when the Twin Grob was so popular I was hired by many commercial operators to haul the big glider from the distribution center in Bluffton, Ohio to their sites. Most operators had no interest in owning a trailer for the beast because they had no plans of taking it apart after the first assembly - it was for rides and training only. The Grob factory had a huge trailer made of aluminum bows and a skin of cheap fiberglass building panels. I'd hauled it many times and signs of fatigue were beginning to show.

I leave the shop at Bluffton one morning with yet another G-103, headed west. Coffee in the cup holder, radio blasting away and the sound of a strong Chevy engine have me lulled into thinking this is another "piece of cake." Suddenly, I feel a slight tug at the wheel, then another a little stronger. I look into the rearview mirror to see the whole side of the trailer skin ripping back. Before I can get stopped I have this huge "elephant ear" dragging in the oncoming lane. Cars on both sides of the road are giving me a wide berth as this "ear" does some seldom-seen aerobatics. I stop and quickly get in the middle of the lane and start pushing this flap back into place. Duct tape is a great invention — I always carry several rolls with me. After an hour or so of rolling the tape under and over the trailer the "elephant ear" is finally pinned in place and I'm underway again.

The destination is Colorado Springs. It's late January and as I approach Colorado the radio is warning of a blizzard forming over the Front Range. I give up any thought of stopping for the night and early the next afternoon arrive at Black Forest Gliderport as light snow is beginning to fall. I catch the owner of the new Grob at the airport but he doesn't even take time to look — with the storm due any minute he

See Ya' at the Airport!

wants to be warm at home when it hits. He tells me the bunkhouse is mine but I must share it with the full-time towpilot. Sure enough, the storm hits with a vengeance, and as the towpilot and I try to see through the snow on the rabbit-eared TV the snow outside is blowing horizontal and drifting high.

It was a fast mover, and by daylight the sky is clear and the air crisp with the temperature near zero. There is nothing to do but make more coffee and read old *Soaring* magazines as I wait for the roads to clear. Around noon the owner shows up in his big "4-wheeler" — he wants to check out his new ship. OK with me, but being a Southern boy I have no interest in being out in that frozen air. And my experience with new owners over the years has taught me to stay out of their way — whatever they want to do is just fine with me.

Soon the owner and another club member have the Grob assembled and the towpilot has the Super Cub out of the hangar with a heater hose stuck into the cowling to warm the engine. The owner goes into a small building and comes out on a riding mower with a plow on the front. He drives out to the runway and begins to push snow. After about five passes he has cleared a narrow track about a thousand feet long. The towplane starts the first time after twenty minutes of heating.

They piddle around for a long time before deciding to fly. One guy hooks up as the towplane taxis into position, then hurries to the rear cockpit and closes the canopy. The engine comes up to speed and the tow is underway. The prop blast picks up the freeze-dried snow like dust and within seconds the two guys in the Grob are in a complete "whiteout." The Super Cub is gathering speed but there is a hump of snow at the end of the plowed section of the runway. Just as it rotates, the wheels hit that hump. In a flash the towplane is on its back. The two guys in the glider are off the ground waiting for the snow to clear so they can see again. WHOMP - the Grob centers the upside-down landing gear of the Cub. This spins the glider out into the heavy snow where it skids and rotates a couple of times before coming to a stop. By now I am running toward the calamity hoping all are all right. I get to the towplane first and see the towpilot digging himself out. "You OK?" I ask. "I think so, what the hell happened?" I give him an

"I don't know" and head for the Grob. Both canopies are open and both guys are unharmed.

The towplane is a complete wreck - not a straight tube on it. The towpilot is stiff but nothing seems broken. We all head back to the office. The first thing the new owner does is call the insurance company. They tell him it is covered and to make arrangements for repair. He hangs up and dials Bluffton. After a long conversation he hands me the phone. It is Jim Short: "We are going to repair the ship — bring it back to Bluffton." I quote a price and he agrees. Late that afternoon I'm back on the road. This is the first and only time that I delivered a new glider, watched it become an old one and took it back to the factory to be repaired, all in less than 24 hours.

* * *

I became a fixture around the Bluffton shop. Many times instead of driving home I would hang around waiting for the next delivery. Jim Short was the head guy. Grob employed Paul Weeden and Robert (Spiderman) Williams as repairman and salesman. We had some great times during this period as business was good, and the jokes were constant.

I got a call for a delivery but it was not a Grob, it was the competitor's ASK-21. Karl Striedieck was the Schleicher dealer at that time. I left Bluffton and arrived at Eagle Field late in the afternoon. Karl showed me the trailer he'd built. It was an open trailer, obviously sturdy, but definitely "Appalachian engineered." We work into the night loading the glider, making modifications where necessary. The ship is going to California and Karl begins to worry about "weather protection." We dig around in the barn and come up with some heavy black plastic sheeting. We cover the fuselage and flying surfaces then wrap them with the famous duct tape.

I'm on the road early the next morning and soon notice a puff of blue smoke every time the trailer takes a bump. I pull over in a rest area and figure out that the heavy steel fenders are too low — the tires are hitting them with each bounce. I call Karl, tell him the problem and suggest I return to base for modifications. Karl says stay where I am until he can get there. OK, time for some good old rest stop machine coffee and a pack of "Nabs." Soon Karl shows up in his van: he has

See Ya' at the Airport!

manhandled his complete welding unit into the side door. We jack up the trailer high enough to avoid burning the tires and Karl takes the torch and cuts a "flap" in the top of both fenders. Soon I am back on the road, watching the tops of the tires appear from time to time though the newly cut "relief valves".

I plan to lay over at Grob with the ASK-21 before heading out again. Within two hours of leaving Eagle Field the plastic covering is starting to shred in the slipstream. By the time I arrive in Bluffton it's a tattered mess. Next morning Mike Shade lets me pull the trailer into the back of the Grob hangar to repair the plastic covering. He warns me that the second man in charge is over from Germany and everyone is on their best behavior.

I climb under the trailer and begin to tape the ripped plastic. I am working away when I hear a voice with a thick German accent ask, "Just what are you doing under there?" I have forgotten about the warning and assume this is some clown off the street. Off the top of my head I answer "I am hiding under here so the boss won't catch me sleeping." I get no response and soon realize the intruder is gone. Suddenly, Mike, Robert, and Paul come bursting through the door in gales of laughter. They can hardly control themselves as I climb out from under, wanting to be a part of the joke.

It ends up I am the joke — I have just been fired. Paul tells me it was a very serious conversation between the German and Jim Short. The thought of me working for Grob has put them into hysterics and being fired makes it even more funny. We sit around for a few minutes laughing and plotting. I decide that I should go to the office, get on my knees and beg Jim Short for my job back in front of the German. I slink into the office with the classic hang-dog look, and my ball-cap in my hands. Jim Short cannot hold a straight face either and both of us break into laughter as the German who is in the other office is listening. Finally, in a laughing voice Jim says loudly, "YOU'RE FIRED - get out of here." I give him a knowing wave and head for the door. I cannot control myself as I go past the German. I duck into his office and say, "I am going to leave on my three-week paid vacation now, thanks." He is not amused. After I left for the Left Coast, Jim and Mike explained my "position" with the company. Even the German guy had to laugh.

Haulin' Glass: The Grob Years

* * *

I did not deliver every Grob twin. I got a call from a commercial operator in New York State asking what the rates were. I quoted him my standard per-mile fee. It was a short conversation as he told me quickly that it was way too much money just to move a glider. I hung up and thought no more of it.

I have another towing job on the hook as soon as the next container gets to Bluffton. I spend several days hanging around waiting for it. One morning an old school bus shows up. Two guys get out and go into the office. Soon Jim comes out and informs us that these guys are here to pick up the last twin Grob in the hangar. It's the guy from New York — he has bought a school bus at auction and plans to put the glider in the back and haul it home. The bus appears to have gone straight from hauling kids to the auction — all the seats are in it, and the special lights and flapping stop sign work flawlessly.

We are whispering among ourselves that this won't work. Just by looking you can see that the wings are way too long to fit into the bus. All of us go about our business with one eye on this operation. They push the fully assembled glider behind the bus, and the first thing that dawns on them is that the fuselage is too wide to go through the rear door. They go in the bus and open the door just to make sure. They must have done this ten times before admitting it was not going to work, no way. We invite them to lunch with us. They say thanks but they are going to need a few things from K-Mart. We come back from lunch and see several of the bench seats out on the tarmac. By mid-afternoon they have the bus gutted and now are looking to improve on the width of the door. We hear the unmistakable sound of a hacksaw on sheet metal as they begin to "modify" the rear of the bus. When we close the hangar at 5:00 they are ready to put the fuselage in, and we agree to help just to see if it will work. With some heaving we get the nose into the back of the bus and start pushing it forward. With the vertical fin still far out of the bus the guy in the front shouts "Stop, stop." It is not going any farther - the nose is against the dash. We help them pull it back out.

Next morning it's obvious these guys have worked through the night. Before the hangar doors are open they ask for help again. They have built a ramp that will take the nose up over the dash and

See Ya' at the Airport!

hopefully allow the fin in. It doesn't work. They resign themselves to the fact that the fin will be in the breeze and begin to consider the wings.

Soon we are again hearing the sound of blade to metal as they slowly remove the whole rear end of the bus. Time to try the first wing. The root is so big that they have to tilt it to get it in. Some ten feet of wing is hanging out back. Now comes the straw that breaks the camel's back - the other wing. We help them get it into the back of the bus but the guys have to go to work, and of course I have no big interest in helping. They spend the whole day trying to fit that Grob into that bus. By closing time they are completely exhausted, and there is no way it is going to work. I am walking out to meet the guys for a beer at the local tavern when I hear a voice behind me say, "Is your price still the same?" I turn and see a completely defeated face looking for a way out of this mess. I tell him that I am waiting for another delivery but I think I have time to do his. I make one policy change: I want my money up front.

Next morning Jim Short has an envelope for me. It has the full amount in cash and a map to the gliderport. Within an hour the plane is loaded and I head out for New York. On Interstate 80 some twenty miles into the Keystone State I see something familiar on the side of the road. I start to slow down when I realize it is the bus. I speed up and change lanes. One of the guys has climbed up on the front and has the hood open. The other is watching the traffic. He spots me and begins to wave frantically. I wave back but never take my foot off the gas. I've got my money, and I'm in a hurry. I have never seen nor heard from that guy again.

* * *

As I continued to transport gliders out of Bluffton I became more and more a fixture around the place. The SSA Convention was coming up in Hartford, Connecticut and Jim wanted Grob to be there in full force. He offered me a free ride and a motel room plus expenses if I'd share the trip with Robert Williams and help get the plane onto the convention floor. I quickly agreed and started helping Robert load the trailer. Not only did we have the Twin Grob, but also all the brochures, booth and boxes of stuff to sell. It was the heaviest trailer I've ever hauled. Because Grob is German naturally they had a German tow vehicle. It was a Volkswagen bus — the air-cooled one that all the hippies love. I think it develops less than 90 hp, and most times cannot get out of its own way. Combine this very weak van with the heaviest trailer and a weather report that includes 6 inches of snow over the next 24 hours and you have all the ingredients for a real road adventure.

Robert and I get up around 4:00 am with two days to get to Hartford. The first snafu happens when we leave the hangar and gas up. It is so cold that Robert puts the gas nozzle in the tank, sets the little clip that keep it flowing, then leaps back into the van. Both of us are huddled in this freezing van which, like all VWs, has no heater. We are warming our hands with paper cups of coffee and grumbling about the hour and the temperature. After what seems like a very long time Robert says the tank should be full and gets out to check. The meter reads 81 gallons, the price is $91 and a river of gasoline runs from the van to the ditch - so much for that wonderful gas mileage Jim had mentioned before we left. We get out on the Interstate with Robert at the wheel. After about five minutes I say, "Buddy, we've got a long trip - let's get moving." Robert informs me that the pedal has been to the metal since we left the service station. The speedometer reads 41mph, and we're on a slight downgrade.

We begin to see snow and soon it is sticking to the road. Two hours out of Bluffton, we've done 74 of the 600 miles to Hartford. The road gets worse and the hills get steeper. Robert has it in first gear chugging up a hill when I decide to lie down in the back. I am not known for being a light fellow and before I can get comfortable Robert is shouting, "GET BACK UP HERE NOW!" What has happened can only be described as a "High-Yo-Silver" maneuver. With the heavy trailer, engine and me in the back, the front wheels left the pavement. Robert was steering wildly with zero result as we rolled down a hill at the blazing speed of

40mph. As I climbed forward the wheels finally contacted the road again.

For the next 30 minutes Robert went between cussing and saying, "We could have been killed." I suggest we pull off and find something to weigh down the front of the van. (Just what we need —

more weight!) We find a building supply store and buy a couple of hundred-pound bags of salt. The weather gets worse and we are seeing lots of cars off the road. I mention to Robert that we are not going fast enough to get hurt in a crash to which he replies with several choice words.

No speed, no heat, no hope - that was our predicament. We knew we would have to keep going no matter what, and that's just what we did. I have never traveled slower or more uncomfortably than I did on that trip. The great thing is that Robert and I worked as a team and that made it a little easier. To this day, when we see each other the greeting is, "Want to drive to Hartford?"

Hauling Grob Twins was the best money I ever made on the road. I saw a great deal of this wonderful country and best of all spent lots of time with my friends. As I said at the beginning, I miss my life on the road something terribly. The memories of all the fun and adventure will never fade.

HAULIN' GLASS: *Trailer Problems*

*O*bviously, not all trailer trips go smoothly. Some that didn't are the subject of this chapter. I've also included some advice on how to avoid problems.

I was working the gate at Littlefield, Texas several years ago when one of the most amazing non-flying incidents I've ever seen happened. It was a contest day with a threat of thunderstorms in the forecast (so what's new?). The start was over and the gate crew was relaxing with soft drinks and a few jokes when we began to hear a terrible noise off in the distance. The road from town is a typical West Texas two-laner with a fairly rough surface. Way down the road we could see a large motorhome approaching and as it got closer the noise got louder. My curiosity got the best of me and I jumped in my van.

As I drive down the fence line the RV turns in and behind it is a Komet trailer that appears to be traveling "Indian papoose" style: there are no wheels under the trailer; in fact there is no axle carriage — the trailer is riding on the hitch and its rear end. Several people are waving their arms to stop the RV. When I get to the scene the "Oh-Oh Squad" has already formed and is pointing at areas of the trailer. The driver gets out, makes a quick inspection and mutters something like "He will kill me," as she sits on the rear bumper of the RV. "Well, this explains the cars that came alongside as I was driving out here," she says. "They were waving and pointing back at the trailer. I kept rolling down the window and shouting 'IT'S A GLIDER'. Now I know why they seemed so frantic."

Her pilot had said that because the weather might mean a landout she should hook up and take the trailer and RV to get gas. Leaving the gas station, she cut the turn short. Motorhomes isolate drivers from the noise of the road and the rear view often leaves a lot to be desired; she felt the drop but assumed she had simply run over the curb. We grabbed the old airport truck and retraced her trip to the gas station. As we turned into the station one of the guys in the back of the truck shouted, "There it is!" The axle lay at the bottom of a cemented ditch. We gathered it up and back at the airport with a butane burner we were able to heat the damaged bolts enough to get them out. We searched the old crop-duster hangar and found four new bolts. Soon the trailer was back on its wheels, a little worse for the wear. Mostly the back end was damaged from the dragging. The crew was greatly relieved. Within 30 minutes the retrieve phone began to ring. I was back at the gate when I saw her head out to fetch her pilot.

I'd been towing gliders about five years when I got a call from a guy down in Florida who wanted a PIK-20 taken to New Mexico. I explained that I was picking up a glider in Atlanta and taking it to LA, but as soon as I got back I'd be available. He told me his customer was in a hurry and he'd have to come up with another solution. Two days later the same guy calls me and says he needs a favor. His sixteen-year-old son is out of school for Thanksgiving and wants to haul the trailer. Naturally Dad is worried about the kid going alone and is asking if I will meet him down on I-10 near Pensacola. I really don't want to do this but the guy makes it worth my time so I agree.

We meet at a shopping center. Dad has followed the kid up from Orlando to get him started. He tells me the kid is doing great and should have no problems. I meet the kid and we shake hands. I've always had trouble communicating with people who wear those earphones and seem to be gyrating to a beat I can't hear. I finally ask him to take the earphones off, which he does reluctantly. The kid is driving a big BMW and the trailer is a Schreder. We agree that we'll stay together. But it's soon obvious that I am going way too slow for this teenager and his powerful car. He drops back then comes racing up on my tail time and time again.

This goes on for a couple of hours when I decide it's time for gas and a drink. After filling up I tell him I am going to stretch for a few minutes. He shouts, "I'll meet you at the next rest area." and takes off. I try to catch him but the next thing I see is the car and trailer going down the on ramp. I won't say what I called this kid as I got into my van and headed out after him.

I'm driving along looking for the rest area when I see a large white object in the hammer lane; it looks familiar but I can't place it. When I pass it I am stunned — it is the left wing of a sailplane! I quickly pull over and walk back to the wing. It is scuffed up but is laying off to the side and has not been hit. I grab the wing root, drag it into the median clear of traffic, note the mile marker and get back in my van. Within three miles I see another white object in the roadway — the right wing. This one has been run over several times and is really not worth stopping for. About twenty miles down the road I see the rest area and my buddy parked along the curb. The Schreder trailer has a one-piece rear door held closed by "dogs." The dogs have shifted and the door is open. The fuselage is halfway out and has been dragging a while — the road has sanded away the tailskid and most of the fiberglass below the rudder and fin.

I walk to the driver's window and see the kid merrily bopping to the sounds of some punk rocker on his earphones. I knock on the glass and get no response. I knock again then try waving my hand over the front windshield. Finally he sees me and without missing a beat gives me a hand signal that I read as "Let's hit the road." I say, "You have a problem." but this does not get through the rolled-up window and the Walkman. "YOU HAVE A SERIOUS PROBLEM." At last the earphones come off and the window comes down.

To this day I wish I could have photographed that kid's face when he walked back to the trailer. He went from a "hip dude" to a crying child in a millisecond. I felt sorry for him but had no real answers. I got him calmed down enough to call home. Dad was angry, mostly with me, but the kid told the truth about what happened and got me off the hook. We secured the fuselage then quietly drove to the next exit and doubled back to retrieve the remains of the two wings. Back at the rest area, I said, "Goodbye, hope you are not in too much trouble," and departed for LA as he began a grim trip back to Florida.

Many years ago I got a job hauling a jet Caproni from Minden to Uvalde. The trailer was heavy but I thought I was okay because it had tandem axles to spread the weight. But its tiny 12-inch wheels and thin tires were soon to prove a real problem. The first sign of trouble came a few miles south of Tonapah, Nevada. I feel a jerk and look in the mirror to see one of the left wheels heading out into the desert. The lugs are okay but of course all the lug nuts are gone. I look for the wheel for 20 minutes or so then abandon the search and get the spare out. I steal a lug nut from each of the other three wheels and head out again. All goes well and I get to a parts store in Kingman, Arizona and pick up more lug nuts. I'm on Interstate 40 about 10 miles east of the Meteor Crater when "boom" — another wheel departs the trailer headed for oblivion.

The trailer will tow on three wheels, but slowly. I drive in the breakdown lane for some four hours before I find a town big enough that they might have a wheel. I pull into an abandoned gas station, disconnect the trailer, take one of the wheels off the left side and start searching. These wheels are Italian and the lug pattern just doesn't match anything American. Finally I find one in a junkyard off a boat trailer that overturned on the Interstate five years before (the guy at the junkyard gave me the history of everything I looked at). I decide that speed combined with heat is throwing these wheels off, so I continue on at 50 mph. It is torture to drive for such a distance at this speed. I get within 50 miles of Uvalde when one more wheel escapes. I do not stop, just slow down some more and keep going. In all the years I towed them, I've never been happier to get rid of a trailer.

These incidents are extreme examples of what can go wrong towing sailplanes. I have driven all types of trailers in all types of weather for a living and I can tell you that paying attention all the time is the only way to get there intact. Here are some trailering tips:

For me, a lot depends on my first impression of the trailer. If it is

See Ya' at the Airport!

obvious that the trailer has been used regularly and maintained I'm more willing to take the seller's word that things are all right. This doesn't mean I don't do a thorough check — I just wait until I get away from the seller so I can do it my way. If a trailer has sat for more than a year then it is important to go much further in checking things. Wheel bearings need looking into. The brake system will need to be checked and rust sanded out of the drums. Everything will need grease, especially the surge brake slide in the trailer tongue.

I look for rust and corrosion on all linkages and in the ball coupler. I carry a "grovel rug" in my van so that I can lie on the ground, check out the undercarriage and grease all fittings. I look for misalignment of the axle itself — driving over curbs and in rough landout fields can knock the undercarriage out of line, meaning that one wheel is behind the other. A clue to this misalignment is "scalloped" tires. Realignment requires the trailer be jacked off the ground and the carriage bolts loosened. I carry a measuring tape with me along with a good set of tools. I use a point on the tongue and triangulate the wheel alignment.

Next come the lights. A light tester is a very necessary tool. My system is to use one hot wire from my van and a ground wire to the trailer. If the trailer has a plug of any kind you start by connecting the hot wire to one of the receptacle pins using alligator clips. If you are lucky some light will shine; if not, you will have to chase the ground. Once I get something working, I start a diagram of which pin is doing what. Most of this is unnecessary for trailer owners — you get it figured out once and it's good for as long as you own the glider.

A close inspection of the trailer fittings and the way the pieces of the sailplane are held in the trailer is important. I remember a multi-time National champion towing a new glider from the port on the East Coast to the 1983 Nationals in Ephrata, Washington. He just hooked up and starting driving. When he pulled the right wing out on the first practice day, about 10 feet of the leading edge had been pounded flat on the floor of the trailer — the support fittings had not been adjusted. During my inspection I always tape the divebrakes closed. The fuselage strap in front of the vertical fin is important — forget to pull this tight and you can damage the top of the fin in the birdhouse. I carry a supply of foam for extra padding. Remember, I'm only

Haulin' Glass: Trailer Problems

delivering a ship — you are going to own it for some time and probably put many more miles on the trailer than I did. Everything that supports and secures the pieces of the ship needs to be checked often.

Recently there have been some failures of the tongue on some modern trailers. These seem to be happening on trailers towed by big RVs. There is a lot of force on any trailer tongue as it takes the heaves and bounces of normal driving. A motorhome is a bigger and heavier hammer than, say, an SUV and will cause more stress. All the years I towed, I carried a "water ballast" inner tube with me. If the tongue weight was wrong I would put the tube in the trailer and fill it until I got the load right. I am not sure what the real solution to the recent problem is but I can tell you that getting down on a "grovel rug" and inspecting carefully is the first step to making sure your glider and trailer do not become an unguided missile out on the Interstate.

Tires are often a sore point. Old tires, especially small ones, tend to dry rot pretty quickly. If you see lots of cracking in the sidewalls, replace the tires. Another problem is underinflated tires — they can get hot and will fail all at once, shredding and slinging the tread into the fender. Usually this blowout is fatal to the fender. At every stop I check the wheel bearings. I do it in a rather crude way: I spit on the cover — if it doesn't sizzle then I will feel for excessive heat. I have heard many stories of pilots and crews watching trailer tires pass them on the highway. This can be caused by overheated bearings or loose lug nuts. Believe it or not, one answer is to grease the thread of the lugs when putting on the lug nuts. This will insure metal-to-metal contact not rust-to-rust or dirt-to-dirt. Over-tightening lug nuts is another way to lose a wheel — it weakens the lugs which can then break under stress. Once one lug breaks, others will soon follow.

I have never had a trailer come off the ball in all the years and miles I towed. The secret was ensuring that the coupler fit the ball. If you get it too tight it can cut and break the ball; too loose and a good bump can take the trailer off the ball. I changed my trailer ball once a year — probably excessive but I was always aware of how much money was following me and how hard a new sailplane is to replace. If you tear one up on the highway, calling the factory for a quick replacement is impossible.

I have always used good old Detroit iron for towing vehicles.

See Ya' at the Airport!

What you want is for the vehicle that you are driving to always be the boss of the operation and the simplest way to guarantee that is to have a heavy tow vehicle. A heavy trailer behind a light tow vehicle can be trouble. There is nothing that will scare you more than going down a hill on the Interstate and suddenly feeling the "sway." It gets worse as soon as you put on the brakes. I know of several people who have ended up with their car on its roof and the trailer and sailplane destroyed.

If you want to tow safely with a smaller vehicle, all your equipment checks become more important. You must be sure the trailer has good tires inflated right, and that the surge brake works (don't even think about it without a good surge brake). Check the overhang from the car's rear axle to the tow ball. If it's small, sway should not be a big deal. A long overhang means the trailer has a lot of leverage and might sway the car badly. Make sure you are happy with the way the tow vehicle and the trailer feel before getting out on a highway or Interstate.

I have been stopped by the Highway Patrol several times for no real reason except they wanted to know what was in the trailer or to make sure things complied with the law. Because the law on tags is different in each state I have never been stopped because I did not have a tag. Usually they want to see how the chains are hooked up, and if all the lights work. I have never been given a ticket because of the trailer, and I never got caught speeding either. Speed is a bad idea when hauling a trailer — excessive speed makes things happen faster and harder.

I'm now retired from towing. I don't miss the trailers but I do miss the open road. The only way I could enjoy it was to know that the sailplane behind me was in a trailer that could take the gaff and was roadworthy. I think the same is true of anyone who wants to enjoy the sport of soaring cross-country.

GYPSY VILLAGE

Gypsy Village is and always has been a mystic place that can form and disappear much like a good thermal. Since my earliest days in the sport of soaring, it was my place to go when the day was over and it was time to lay back, pop a cool one, and spend time with friends.

The original Gypsy Village was at the end of a seldom-used dead-end dirt road on the outskirts of the Chester airport. The airport was built during WW-II and they had moved a lot of dirt on the west end. This small mountain soon became overgrown with brambles, skinny pines, and kudzu. It was a peninsula surrounded by a drainage ditch and there was only one way in and out. It was a perfect place for a young man to be himself in the late 60s.

At this time in my life I was trying to make sense of what I was doing, where I was going, and most of all why. After several years of trying to become a contributing member of society by holding a full-time job, being responsible and planning for the future, I realized I was not happy. When I finally made the decision to give it up and try something new, I went from a coat-and-tie, clean-shaven textile salesman to a smiling, laughing, carefree and fun-seeking ne'er-do-well.

Of course this was the lifestyle I was looking for and the only problem was that I needed money to maintain it. I began to pick up odd jobs like painting and house repair, but these were too much work and not enough money. I'd always had a talent for auto repair and I had a friend with a shop; if you are good at car repair you can pretty much work when you want – like a nurse or an electrician, you'll never be unemployed. I got good at "fixin' cars" and it was my main income for more than 25 years.

Now with a modest income established I was able to really chase my interest in soaring. As time went on I realized that the cost of flying was going to limit all the other things I wanted to do. I wanted to travel most of all and was frustrated in all my attempts to do so. Traveling really demanded money.

Like a divine intervention I was asked to work at the first sanctioned soaring contest at Chester, South Carolina in 1969. It was after this contest that I realized that just maybe there was a way to use my abilities to get where I wanted to be. For this contest I worked the "window": a setup for verifying the start height of competing gliders. It was at the site of this that Gypsy Village was founded.

Competition soaring was introducing me to some of the finest people I had ever met. They were successful, friendly, and appreciated what I was doing for the contest. I was really enjoying myself, but the pressure of staying on my best behavior got a little tough toward the end of the day. I would retreat to what would soon become Gypsy Village for some down time.

I was meeting several folks near my age who were crewing or working in the contest. As we became friends I found out that they were also looking for something to do after the sun went down. The isolation of the airport and the fact that most of us stayed up long after the pilots were sound asleep were the catalysts for Gypsy Village.

The first person I let in on the secret was Sam Lyons. Sam was crewing for Gren Siebels and hopping into any glider someone would let him fly. At 6 foot 5 inches Sam is a big guy, and like me loved a good laugh. He had been a teacher and coach at a private school in Atlanta and like me was trying something new. He was a national champion aircraft modeler and had just opened a hobby shop in Doraville, Georgia named *Historical Hobbies*. I also built models and our first conversation took place while I was hand-launching a balsa glider.

Sam was looking for something to do after hours. After a contest cookout, Sam and I retreated down that dirt road for some R and R. April can be cool in the South and that night we built a small fire and sat around shooting the bull – and forming a friendship that has lasted to this day. Sam met one of the pilots' daughters and invited her to Gypsy Village. He said I should take a shot at finding someone to share the fire with. Unknown to us, the girls we approached were spreading the word among the younger crew that there was a place on the airport where they could get away from parents and prying eyes. That night the village had a dozen citizens; several brought tents and sleeping bags. As the week went on we gained more and more gypsies and soon some parents were asking, "Where are all of you going at night?"

Sam and I knew that if the secret were exposed, the village would die. The next night we had an impromptu village meeting. After much discussion Sam was declared "King of the Gypsies," and I was given the title of "Fuehrer." The first thing we decided was that we would never reveal the location to any outsider. The second rule was simple: anything that happened in the village never left the village. Since that time these have been the only laws that rule Gypsy Village.

As King of the Gypsies, Sam was in charge of all entertainment. No matter what we were doing Sam would come up with a way to make it entertaining. I remember the famous steak-eating contest. We had bought steaks to cook over the fire that night and found we had one extra. Sam came up with the idea that whoever ate their steak first got the extra one. I have never seen steak eaten like it was that night. I remember looking up as I was gulping down that meat and seeing Sam sneak that last steak off the grill. There were lots of "Oh no you don'ts" but Sam escaped the grasps and started chomping. Sam was full of pranks and gags and over the years we have collaborated on many, both on and off the airport. If you happen to meet him just mention my name – I promise you some great stories.

The parties would run late some nights and I can remember being awakened by the ring of the field phone as the contest start gate was setting up and looking for me to operate the window. I had missed all the morning activities including the pilots meeting. (I only wish I could sleep like that now.)

One spring I showed up with a couple of girl friends from the city. I had convinced them that they needed a break from the hustle and bustle of city life. I told them of bright sunny days – they could get a tan and claim they had actually gone to the beach. I talked about being under the stars at night and how quiet and beautiful Gypsy Village was. They were waitresses in a local bar and getting away did appeal to them. At the last minute they agreed to pack up sleeping bags and head for Chester with me. Once there they did get into the contest and were enjoying the fun. They especially enjoyed the nightlife in the village.

One afternoon while I was chasing a break in the field phone wire the two girls decided to work on their tans. I had a mattress in the back of my old pickup truck and I took the camper shell off so they could lie in the bed without having to be on the ground. It was just the three of us at the village and with me gone they decided to sunbath nude. The truck was perfect for this – when they were prone no one on the ground would even know they were in the truck. I came back to the window and shouted up the hill that I would be working for a while to which they said "Great."

The launch got underway and I was busy trying to get communication between the gate and the window working. Cloudbases were below 2,000 ft, gliders were struggling and there were some relights. With all this action I was not paying any attention to the girls. Over the field phone Rusty called to say that a couple of gliders were low right over the window. I looked up and, yes, they were low and appeared to be struggling.

About ten minutes later Rusty calls again and points out that it looks like all the gliders in the contest are right over the window. I don't think anything of it until Rusty mentions that on the radio the pilots are talking about something they see on the ground near the window. I tell Rusty there is nothing going on up here. Suddenly, I hear a car coming down the dirt road at a fast clip. It stops in a cloud of dust and out steps Lucy Giltner. I'm amazed: this proper Southern lady is the last person I expect to see in Gypsy Village – I'm surprised she even knows where it is. Lucy gets out of the car and goes straight to the pickup. The girls sit up and at last I realize what the problem is. As they are hastily dressing, Lucy is headed in my direction: "Young man, you are in a *lot* of trouble!" She turns, gets back in the car, and drives away. I look up where that huge gaggle had just been and there is not a glider in sight. So much for keeping Gypsy Village a secret.

Over the years Gypsy Village moved from airport to airport; the populace changed but all who camped there stuck to the rules. Who drank too much, who was rolling Hollywood smokes, and who romanced who are all secrets never to be revealed. I know of two children who were conceived in Gypsy Village. I took one of them along on a summer of soaring when he turned 13 (that summer was more than 13 years ago).

Gypsy Village was the birthplace of SCUM: Sailplane Crew Union Members. I was appointed Dictator for Life of this loose group of question-askers and troublemakers. In those days you had to earn your union card, and my decisions were final. Sometimes we would have ceremonies in Gypsy Village and sometimes I would just hand them their card after a contest was over. We had four simple rules:

1. During the contest, the pilot is always right.

2. If the pilot is wrong, refer to rule #1.

3. In case of a landout, the pilot owes the crew a steak dinner.

4. On non-contest days the pilot is always wrong and pays for everything.

On occasion we would declare a mock strike and read our grievances during one of the morning pilots meeting. Everyone joined in the fun and it was all done for laughs.

As I have grown older and my place in soaring has changed, Gypsy Village has unfortunately pretty much faded into the past. Age and time are destroyers of so much. SCUM has become a respected entity supporting the US Soaring Team through the sale of T-shirts, jackets, and the famous Scumbag tote. The name SCUM offended some folks and I used to take pride in that fact. Nowadays when I see

Gypsy Village

some of the veteran crews wearing those T-shirts proudly I sometimes think a new name might be better.

I will forever remember those wonderful nights of friends, drinks, and laughter. Skinny-dipping in the lake at Adrian, climbing the abandoned rail cars behind the Ephrata airport, driving with the headlights out down the abandoned runways of Hobbs – all are memories of wonderful fun. There are many more, but the unwritten laws of Gypsy Village will not allow me to elaborate. Best of all were the lasting friendships formed in the twilight of a racing day.

THE SIBERIAN EXPRESS

Most of my sailplane towing experiences were routine. I was proud of my record delivering gliders safely and on time. Of course, not all trips went smoothly, and as you'd expect, the difficult ones often made for the best stories.

Coming out of Warrenton, Virginia with a single-place *Lark* in tow, my destination was Minden, Nevada. It was the first of the year and though the air was cold it looked like an easy trip; just lots of time in the seat and a lot of coffee to keep warm.

I made it to Nashville, and spent the evening with the Tom McFarlane family. We were sitting around the TV, talking and laughing, when the weather report came on. I listened as the weather guy said the usual and pointed to the map. It showed a front to the north and for the first time I heard the name Siberian Express. The prediction was that it would get to the lower states in 36 hours, so I relaxed a little and headed for bed with plans to get an early start just to make sure it missed me as I headed west.

The Siberian Express

I got a great start next morning; it was sunny and cold. I crossed Tennessee and was coming into Arkansas when I noticed that the overcast was getting thicker. I stuck my hand out the window: the temperature was definitely dropping.

Twenty miles from the Oklahoma border it began to snow. Now my usual procedure when towing in snow is to slow way down and if the road goes slick I forget about driving and wait for improvement. I was sticking to my plan, but the snow was sticking to the road faster than I'd ever seen. In thirty miles the visibility was down to four feet, and my speed was four mph.

Time to look for a place to land. As I crept down the interstate, above me appeared a sign barely readable in the blowing snow: Sallisaw, Oklahoma, Next Exit. By now I couldn't tell the road from the ditch, but with a little luck I found the exit ramp. Still moving slowly and really worried that I would have to stop due to no visibility, I finally saw a sign glowing red off to the left. All it said was "Motel."

I pulled in with the rear tires slipping under the load of sailplane and trailer, and parked under a sign that said "Office." The comment that the little lady made when I walked in should've given me a hint of what was to come. She looked at her dog, one of those good-for-nothing, curly-haired types that you can hold in one hand, and said, "Oh good, Fluffy, we're not going to be skunked tonight."

I asked for a room, and was told the price was $18.45. Along with my key to room 12 and my receipt, I was given a rather worn-looking portable heater. Little did I realize that we were to become the best of friends over the next few days.

I unlocked the door to number 12 and before me was a room that had survived the Great Depression, although not very well. The furniture was worn and shabby, the walls were a tired tan color, made worse by a single bare light bulb glaring from a fixture in the ceiling. The bed looked like a large catcher's mitt which I soon discovered had only one sweet spot. The TV was an ancient black-and-white Motorola; the screen produced more snow than the Siberian Express could muster just outside the door. I was taken aback by the plumbing fixtures, but after running the hot water faucet for several minutes, I could notice a slight difference between the water flowing from it and the near-frozen liquid available from the cold water tap.

See Ya' at the Airport!

The Siberian Disaster was really howling outside now, and a glance out the frost-covered window proved that trying to go anywhere with a van and a glider was an idiot's folly. "Oh well," I said to myself, "It's only one night. I can stand anything for one night." After removing my coat I realized that the room wasn't much warmer than it was outside. I stepped over to the in-room heater which was nothing more than an old air conditioner with a heat button on it. I hit high. After waiting for a long time I realized a match could generate more heat than that poor, dilapidated machine. Now I was thankful for that portable heater: soon after I plugged it in, I did notice an improvement in temperature. The drawback was that the portable could only generate a comfort zone about four feet in front of it, which meant that, like Mary's little lamb, everywhere I went that heater was sure to go.

With some program coming from somewhere inside the snowy mass that was on the screen, and my new-found friend, the portable heater, glowing away on the little table beside my bed, I climbed into that catcher's mitt for a restful night in Sallisaw. I awoke for reasons that soon became obvious: I was as cold as I had ever been in my life. My little buddy sat lifeless beside me in the freezing dark. The Siberian Express had killed the electricity.

I dressed with everything I had in my overnight bag, but it wasn't enough, and after much thought and shivering I decided that I needed to retrieve my down jacket and blanket from the van. The trip to the van was a lesson in snow survival, as by now the drifts were up to the door handles, making the doors very difficult to open. I finally grabbed the coat and blanket through a half-opened door and made my way back through the howling wind and blowing snow. Back in my lovely room I put on the coat, spread the blanket and re-entered my Beauty-rest bed. I piled everything else on top of me and tried to sleep, but all I could do was shiver and cuss. A true miracle occurred as I lay there being frozen to death: my little buddy the heater suddenly came to life with that wonderful red glow. To this day I believe that the Almighty restored the power – I cannot imagine any crew trying to work in that storm.

From the dull light in the frosted windows I could tell that morning had finally arrived. I got up and took my first daylight look

The Siberian Express

at the Siberian Express. I was hoping that this storm from hell would weaken and die, but it just wasn't happening. The note posted on the door warned checkout time was 11:00 a.m., and as the hour slowly rolled around it was obvious that I was doomed to another night in the Twilight Zone. I was getting hungry, so with much procrastination I finally attempted to get to the office to pay my next $18.45 and see if there was anywhere I might get a bite to eat.

She took my money, and answered my question about a nearby restaurant: "Sally's the only place within walking distance. But she's been closed for three years now." Luckily for me I had some bran flakes and canned tuna fish left over from my last attempt to get slim and eat right. I retrieved the stuff from the van and after eating bran flakes out of the box, and a couple of cans of tuna opened with a pocket knife, I remembered why I had given up the diet: this stuff just doesn't taste good.

As morning turned to afternoon, real boredom set in and I remembered that I had a model airplane kit in the van. I set up on the little night-stand table and began to work on the model, but soon cold hands really began to bother me. My little buddy the heater did a great job but he was restricted by the length of his cord. I decided that giving up the TV was not going to be much loss, so with my trusty pocket knife I cut the power cord to the TV and spliced it into the heater's lifeline. Now I could move freely around the room with my little pal and his longer cord. He sat close by as I cut and glued my model together. As the afternoon passed into evening we became even closer friends.

That night, the temperature dropped to 6 below and the wind increased – this was truly an awesome storm. By morning the snow had stopped and the wind was quieting. The sky was brighter, and by 10 o'clock I could see 18-wheelers slowly moving west on the interstate a half-mile away. Maybe today is the day I escape from purgatory and return to the world of the living. Time to make the big leap. The starter on the van groans as the cold engine turns over. At last the sound of a fully choked engine is music to my ears, and with some rocking motion the whole rig breaks loose from its frozen prison and we are rolling out of the parking lot onto the road, shaking snow and ice as we go.

See Ya' at the Airport!

I don't have much good to say about my ordeal, and I will always shiver at the words Siberian Express. But me and that little heater really did become the best of friends, and I hoped the little lady and Fluffy wouldn't mind if my electric buddy rode shotgun with me at least until July.

GOOFY GATE

There is an old saying: "Nothing is certain except change." In the thirty-five years I have been around sailplane racing, this has certainly applied – just about everything has changed except for the fact that the pilots have to fly cross country and go fast to win. Of course, not every change is a success. Some that weren't are presented here.

The reason I am in this sport has nothing to do with flying. It has to do with a simple radio transmission when a sailplane crossed the start line. Saying, "Mark" as the sailplane passed overhead let the pilot know he had been seen and gave him the opportunity to set his clock. With that one change in the way things were being done, I became known as the guy to do the Gate. From that beginning I have seen sailplane competition grow and change in every way.

Turnpoint Control
Until the early 1960s, confirming that a pilot had made a task

meant that a two-man team had to go to each turnpoint with a set of four black-and-white panels. The panels were laid out be- hind a hangar so pilots had to round the hangar in order to see and note the pattern of the panels. A sharp panel crew changed the configuration every 15 minutes, and kept a record of the changes. This system meant that the task had to be decided early in the morning so the crews could drive to the turnpoints and get set up. In those days a good pair of binoculars in the cockpit was mandatory.

The change that put an end to this was the rule that required pilots to carry a camera and take photos of the designated turnpoints, in sequence. This meant things like pre-start photos and post-flight film developing and evaluation, but getting proof of turnpoints became much easier. (Of course, with this change we heard the same arguments from pilots that always come up when a new system comes into the sport.)

With a camera in every cockpit, many began to think of ways to use it to get a start time: a lot of people were attracted by the idea of using the camera to eliminate the ground crew manning the gate. This was the beginning of what I call the "goofy start" period in sailplane racing.

Ground Clocks

It really came to a head when the U.S. was awarded the 1983 World Championships, to be flown at Hobbs, New Mexico. I was proud of my start gate system – it was well tested and I knew I could handle the load of a world championship as long as I got the crew I wanted. But when they told me that they were going to use an experimental "ground clock" in the Championships I bowed out of having anything to do with it. Of course I was hoping it would not happen but as the contest got closer it became obvious that the ground clock was going to be tried.

Even though I was having nothing to do with the ground clock most folks did not know that and they associated me with start gates. So I began to receive letters with ideas on how to make a ground clock.

The first involved getting one of those bank clock signs that shows the time as you drive by. This guy's idea was to take the sign to the

See Ya' at the Airport!

airport and turn it toward the sky. As the pilots flew over all they would have to do is photograph the "bank clock" for their start time, then head out on course. I can remember going downtown to the main Bank America building and realizing I could not tell you what time it was from a block away, much less from 5 or 6 thousand feet. The guy suggesting this had done no research into what bank would be willing to give up their clock or how to get power to it in the middle of the airport.

The next letter had a completely different approach. This guy said that we should get a kiddie carnival train, set the track in a circle, and drive the train at a set speed around the circle. Every time the train made a complete circle another car would be added. I actually wrote the guy back and asked, "Do I put the car on while the train is running or will it need to be stopped?" Of course he never mentioned where we could get the train and the track, or how we would get them to Hobbs.

All plans were a version of making a clock on the ground big enough to show up in a photograph. One person even suggested a huge clock with the hour and minute hands being moved by an army of kids. Obviously this guy had never dealt with a herd of kids — can you imagine getting the kids to pull those hands slowly in a circle under the hot sun? Maybe in ancient Egypt this clock could have worked, but not in modern times with modern kids.

The clock that was actually used at Hobbs consisted of a tractor with the throttle set, circling a row of panels. The panels were opened and closed according to the time and the tractor told the minutes. The clock ran for four hours and was manned by a team of 12 volunteers. Pilots were able to start when they wanted at the height they wanted. There would be no radio calls, so competitors would not know when each other pilot started.

Unfortunately the first contest day saw the fleet get above 12,000' AGL: with small fixed-lens cameras the photographs were pretty much unreadable. At those heights, what you saw was mostly the curvature of the earth and lots and lots of scrub desert. Many on the first day of the World Championships were scored on the time they called back in.

The manpower and equipment it took to operate a ground clock pretty much doomed it to the dustbin of soaring history. It was tried a few more times with everything from airport riding mowers and cars to go-carts. No one ever seemed to be able to drive around the circle at the same speed. Sailplane trailers were often used to mark the changes in time. I can remember how in one pilots meeting at a Regional contest in New Castle a pilot was very enthusiastic about the ground clock and was telling the group how it should be done. He described how trailers would be lined up and moved and rotated to give the accurate time. When he was finished I set him up by asking him if we could use his trailer. His answer was classic: "Well, no — I might need it on a landout." He suggested using the other pilots' trailers. After a couple of trailers were banged together during practice clock operation we quickly returned to the old familiar gate.

Raising the Start Height

I realized that I needed to work on improving the gate we were using. The biggest problem was that pilots were required to cross the start no higher than 3,300' AGL and this had always made the first thermal the most important of a contest day. If the start height could be raised the first thermal would be less critical and speeds would be faster.

Lanier Frantz was kind enough to purchase a pair of WW2 German 88-mm spotting binoculars and issue them to me. These gave the gate the ability to see the contest number under a wing at a height of 5,000' AGL. With a little practice, a crew of sharp-eyed teenagers could spot gliders just as well as at the old height.

The Speed-Limited Gate

Another problem with the old 3,300' gate was the speeds at which pilots and gliders went through on a good day. Converting height to speed and back again was the name of the game — the faster you dove through the gate the higher you were for the start of the first leg. Karl Striedieck took this simple principal to the extreme at the 15-Meter Nationals in Hobbs in 1978. Karl took the wingtips off of his ASW-17, giving him the 15-meter span he needed — and a *very* strong wing. On the good contest days Karl would come to the Initial Point as high as he possibly could and then go into a terminal-velocity dive until he heard the "mark." With a high-G pullup, Karl could gain several hundred feet on his competitors coming out of the gate.

Many thought this was dangerous and of course wanted to stop Karl from getting that wonderful advantage right at the start. The next year the contest was at Ephrata, Washington, and the club there decided to implement a speed-limited gate. It was set up so that when a pilot crossed the IP a pip sound was heard over 123.3. If a second pip was heard before the sailplane crossed the start line, it meant the pilot had stayed within the speed limit. The biggest problem was the fact that the window operation was in charge of the speed and the start line controlled the gate, and they were far apart, communicating by radio. On several occasions a pilot would hear the pip followed by his call sign and "proceed." If the pilot was careful and got the speed right he might be too high over the gate and many of the transmissions were very confusing. The pilot might hear the pip then the window say, "Good start" only to hear the start line say "Bad try – too high." "Bad try" is not something a racing pilot really wants to hear. There were lots of curse words uttered over 123.3, both in the air and on the ground.

George Moffat won every contest day at Ephrata, mainly because he is the best but also because he pretty quickly defeated the speed-limited gate. George would do much as Karl had done except go to terminal velocity. He would stall-fall for some distance until he had the time limit beat and then scream through the gate for a start, followed by a pullup. The speed-limited gate went the way of all the others and is now collecting dust in some dark corner of the contest-history closet.

The Coded Start

Another problem often mentioned was "leeching" – a bunch of pilots looking to start just behind one of the hot names and follow him around the task. If a pilot could start without others knowing it, maybe leeching would be curbed. This was the idea behind the coded start.

Each morning I assigned each pilot a code name or number to be used when calling at the IP. With the help of my trusty gate crew we would write the code on a small piece of paper, fold it, and put the real contest number on the outside. These slips of paper were given to

Goofy Gate

each pilot during the morning pilots meeting. It worked okay, but no one was really tricked — everyone knows the radio voices of the other pilots. It was really a hoot to hear pilots trying to disguise their voices with mumbling and high-pitched girly words.

With the powerful binoculars in use, we even tried a system with the code and the pilot simply giving "three clicks" at the IP. This system also worked but was a much heavier load on the gate crew. Soon we were back to the standard IP calls with the 5,000' AGL maximum start height.

The "Pole" Start

One of my all-time favorite attempts at "fixing" the gate was tried at Hobbs once. The idea was for the pilot to fly around a pole. That's right, around a pole. The "gate operator" would sit in a chair alongside the pole (in this case a telephone pole on the airport) and as the sailplane "went around" he got a start. Now on the ground a telephone pole is a huge object. In the air at 5,000' a vertical telephone pole is non-existent. What seems perfectly plausible on the ground is impossible from the air.

I was not the gate operator at this contest — I was asked to be the launch master. The guy who was the operator was also the inventor and had decided that no one in the air would be given directions even if it was clear they were going to miss the gate. The "cussing" over 123.3 was the worst I had ever heard and once when I looked up there were at least six gliders in the general area doing "donuts," trying to go around that pole. Needless to say the next day we returned to the old familiar gate and I was reinstalled as gate operator.

Clock Cameras

The next attempt to get away from the ground-operated gate was the clock camera. It was simple enough — all a pilot had to do was fly to the designated start point and take a picture of the photo target. When he did, his clock camera automatically put an imprint of the time on the film.

When you take time control out of the hands of the organizers and put it the hands of the individual pilots you are asking for trouble. Instead of using one clock to time all the competitors you are now dealing with 65 different clocks, all set differently and operated by 65 different pilots. This is a real disaster in the making for any contest organization. This system was used in many countries in the late 1980s but not in the United States. The SSA Contest Rules Committee required the cameras, but by the time we were ready to use them we were already getting unfavorable reports.

The clock camera system became more and more complicated as its use increased. By the time it was used in the World Championships, what it took to get a start was pretty amazing. It consisted of lots of security photographs of a master clock to insure the accuracy of each individual camera's clock. If all the steps were not done right a pilot could end up with a zero score. On one contest day some 11 pilots got zero because of problems with the camera system.

The clock camera was killed at the 1993 World Championships in Borlange, Sweden when a Hungarian pilot devised a way to hold the time from being imprinted on the film until a hidden button was pressed. The pilot would photograph the start point and then sometime later, out on course, he would press the magic button. Saving 10 or more minutes gave him some great speeds. Suddenly he was winning the contest.

The Championship officials could not believe this pilot was doing so well and decided to set a trap. For the next day's start point they selected a traffic "roundabout" in the local village. It was the return of the ground clock: the officials parked a car in different locations at different times around the circle, and kept a log. It worked, and the pilot's cameras were confiscated and examined. The cheating was discovered and the pilot disqualified from the Championships.

GPS and Flight Recorders

The United States stayed with the "American Gate" and its 5,000' start height until the late 1990s when GPS proved beyond all doubt it was the way to start, and also to control the contest in every way. Not only did the starts improve, but with GPS flight recorders came new tasks and better scoring.

We are well into the new era of competition soaring and the future looks very bright to me. From the Competition Director to the Scorer to the pilots flying the course, GPS has made everyone's job easier. I

Goofy Gate

like the new system very much and think it is part of the reason we are seeing Regional and National contests fill up with waiting lists now.

I must admit I miss the old Gate in many ways — after all, it was my kingdom for so many years. I also know that the system we use today is much better. Competition soaring will continue to grow and change. I am sure the future is full of new ideas and new ways of doing things. Some of the ideas will be wonderful and promote the Sport. Others will be wonderful for their goofiness and their "out of the box" thinking. One thing is for sure: I hope I am there to see them in action.

RHYME OR REASON

At sailplane races, some familiar scenes can be very entertaining. One of my favorites is the pilot who after a long layoff from racing decides it's time to get back in the swing of things.

For many pilots, the hardest part of returning to sailplane racing is convincing the family that this will be a great vacation for everyone. Telling his wife that the motel will be perfect and the kids will love the pool is only the start of a deception that will come to haunt him once underway. What our pilot has done is convince his family that an abandoned airport, somewhere in the Midwest, will be the site of their greatest adventure.

After a long, hot trip they arrive at this alleged soaring Mecca. The pilot leaps out of the driver's seat and immediately begins to shake hands with everyone in sight. Talking about sailplanes and racing, the smile on his face and the sparkle in his eyes indicates to the family that he indeed has arrived in soaring heaven. The look on their faces is one of amazement and disbelief. This is an old World War II

Navy airbase that hasn't seen a salute or a broom since Truman dropped the bomb. The buildings are dirty and windblown, with paint peeling off the window frames. To one side of the main building are several old cars that have sat there so long trees are growing up through the wheel wells and broken windshields. Off in the distance, an old Cessna lies in a drainage ditch, overturned and crumpled by the winds of the plains. In every corner, trash and tumbleweeds swirl in the wind as if they, too, would like to escape this place.

The pilot has met most of the folks on the ramp, and now has returned to his bewildered brood. One of the kids looks at dad with a face of innocence: "Dad, are you sure this is the place?" "Sure it is! Come on, let's go into the old tower building and register." With dad in the lead the gang heads for the tower. The old steps are pitted and broken, and there is not a pane of glass in the doors. Once inside the children reach for mom's hand out of instinct as they see it's even worse in there: trash is everywhere; old tables and chairs are scattered around with no indication that anyone has used them in years. Bare light bulbs dangle from useless fixtures, and ceiling tiles droop and sag from the exposed beams. As they climb the steps leading to the registration office, one of the kids points to a small bird flying out of a broken window. Those streaks down the walls are not old paint, but something the birds have been working on for a long time. The smell is hard to describe: somewhere between a toxic outhouse and a pair of old tennis shoes.

I must admit I am now waiting near their crew vehicle to hear the conversation as they return from registration. I am always entertained the most by the wife's comments. Few of them can be printed in this story, but from the look on her face this is going to be a very long contest.

Next morning they reach the airport early. Again the pilot jumps out of the car with enthusiasm; his crew seems to be a little less energetic. The motel was not the vacation dreamland dad had described. Neon-lighted trim and half-buried auto tires make up the décor. The flashing sign "Pool" should have said "Horse Trough." The rooms are small, and made smaller by the little TV in the corner. The shower is misnamed: it should be "the dribble." All this plus the main line of the Southern Pacific less than 100 feet out back have made for an interesting first night.

It's the first practice day – time to get down to the business of winning this little outing. The trailer is open and the wingstands are in place. As the fuselage rolls out it is obvious that the plane has not seen the light of day since last season. A layer of dust covers the top of the fuselage and wings. Mouse footprints can be seen over the canopy, and cobwebs droop between the pitot tube and the fin. Dad begins to bark orders. *Lift! Lift! Back! More back! OK, jiggle!* are commands that can be heard only in this sport. Finally, the ship is assembled and the pilot is busy with details as the crew, with sweat on their faces, retires to the shade of the car. "Mom, can we go back to the motel?" "Not yet honey," as she looks at her watch: it's a little after nine AM. Dad appears behind the car with the trunk open, asking, "Do you know what we did with the wing tape?" Then comes the order that will haunt the crew for the rest of the contest: "Honey, find out where we can fill the water bags."

Filling six 5-gallon water bags from leaking low-pressure hoses is nothing compared to lifting them into the trunk of the car. Then back at the tie-down, hauling them out and trying to hold them higher than the wings in order to fill the ballast tanks. Just as the last bag is going into the wing Dad hollers "*Stop!*" The son swings the bag to the ground with a great sigh of relief as dad frantically jerks pads and parachute from the cockpit. Over the winter a rather large leak seems to have developed – the cockpit has turned into a spring of ballast water. "OK, we've got to take the wings off and find this leak." The moans are loud, and the smell of crew rebellion is in the air.

Under growing protest and sullen silence, the sailplane is finally declared airworthy. Grid time is close and there is the last-minute rush to get to the runway. "Mom, *please*, can we go to the motel? I'm hungry!" "Listen kids, I wish we all could go right now, but dad needs us to help him fly in the contest." "I don't care" comes from the youngest sitting in the back of the car. Mutiny is now a real threat to this fragile alliance. "Son, do you want to run my wing?" "No dad, I want to get out of this heat and get something to eat."

Finally the towplane rolls up and the towrope is attached. As dad disappears down the runway there is a feeling of real relief among the crew. With orders to stay on the airport and be ready to hook up and head out, the crew returns to the tie-down area. With most of the pilots in the air and out on task, now the crew can get a bite to eat, cool off, rest and, best of all, meet some of the other crews. This is when crews have a chance to mingle, and the kids begin to make friends. Crews are the support that makes the race possible. This common thread makes for friendships that can last a lifetime, and which bring so many back year after year to subject themselves to this unique form of abuse.

As the wife sits in the car reading the book she promised herself on this vacation and the kids are throwing a Frisbee with new-found friends, a sailplane flies over, low and fast – time to move out near the runway to catch the wing, and put the tail dolly on. Dad is out of the cockpit talking excitedly, waving his hands in the air describing every turn and thermal during the flight. They snap the tail dolly on with no problems and head for the tie-down. Dad's elation seems to overtake them, and soon the kids are asking questions, and mom actually has a smile on her face.

Sailplane back in the box and all equipment stowed, the gang heads for the scoring office. Even though it's a practice day folks are standing around, beers in hand, looking at the score sheet posted on the window, talking and laughing. After a while a new sheet is posted. Dad moves up to the window and stares intently, then backs away with a smile on his face. He has finished sixth for the day – not bad when you look who he is running against. He comes back to the crew with the good news, and they share his happiness. As they stand on the ramp enjoying the end of the day, someone comes up and says, "A bunch of us are going into town to the Pizza Barn, would you like to join us?" In unison the kids shout "*Yes!*" and head for the car. Dad says, "We'll meet you there." Back at the motel the kids are in the pool, and even though it is small they are all getting wet. Several other contestants and crews are staying at the motel and many of them are sitting around the pool. With a cool drink in hand and a common interest, the conversations go on until dark, and the glue that will bind them all to this sport is oozing everywhere.

They came to the sailplane race a family, but now they are a team with dad as the hero, mom as the crew chief, and the kids with their important jobs to make sure dad has a chance to do well. Time is compressed in a championship. Friendships grow quickly and the social life is intense. No matter how dad does, his team is there to cheer his triumphs and console his failures. The world they came from seems far away as sailplanes cross the finish line and line up to land. The kids have become expert crew, and can tell you who the movers and shakers are in this race. They can spout the rules to anyone who asks and explain the nuances of start strategy. The oldest daughter thinks the crew for "AZ" is cute, and the youngest boy wants his new buddy to come home with him. Mom has it all running so smoothly that the trials of the first day are long forgotten.

For some 30 years I have watched this transformation too many times to count, and it is one of my favorite parts of sailplane racing. Maybe, just maybe, this *is* the best vacation they could ever have, and the great adventure Dad promised so long ago.

Charlie with Susanne Moffat in the 1980's.

Officiating the wedding ceremony of Micky and Charlie "Lite" Miner on the ramp at Mifflin, Pennsylvania, 2003.

With Tommy Beltz, 1975.

Giving an airport tour to a group of school children in Mifflin, Pennsylvania in 2000.

Kidding around with Tina and Josie Bearden during the 2003 Sports Class Nationals on Harris Hill, one year before his second kidney failure.

With National Champions Don Pollard and George Moffat at the 1996 Seniors in Seminole Lake, Florida.

Influences: Klaus Holighaus (top left), Johann Kuhn (top right), and Dick & Angie Schreder (bottom).

A major influence in Charlie's life, Gren Seibels.

His favorite pastime: driving a cart packed with kids around the airport. Uvalde, Texas 2004, with the Buchanan girls.

Gypsy Village was the birthplace of S. Sailplane Crew Union Members.

'Red Baron Charlie'
Photograph by Chris Woods

Uvalde, Texas 2000.

THE JOKESTER

Like all offbeat societies, soaring has its characters. Sailplane racing involves not only man and machinery, but the personalities of the participants. Having left the humdrum of daily life behind for a week or two, parts of their personalities emerge that are magnified by this short but intense period. This chapter tells about one outstanding example.

Mahlon Weir was certainly a character. In his daily life he ran an auto electrical repair business in Boca Raton, Florida. He had a wonderful wife and three beautiful children. He owned a home on a small airport where he flew for fun, and enjoyed every appearance of normalcy.

A few things around the house gave him away: He loved windmills, but did not use them in the time-honored way. Windmills have pumped water on countless farms for centuries. Mahlon spent a great deal of time finding new ways to use this ancient form of energy. He had designed a windmill to saw firewood while he was at work.

The Jokester

Each morning, Mahlon would lay a log in a trough, slide it under the windmill, and engage the saw. Of course it would only saw one log a day, but as he said, "One a day keeps the cold away."

Mahlon loved all types of flying, and especially the atmosphere of a soaring contest. He flew in several 1-26 Championships, and towed at many Regional and National races. He flew a Maule, and the minute it appeared in the air over a contest site, the place took on a different feel.

For many years Chester, South Carolina, was the site of the year's first contest. It was held around Easter, and was known as the "Unofficial Nationals" because of the caliber of pilots who came to shake off winter and practice for the upcoming summer races. As at all airports, the politics could get pretty heated at times. It was April of 1978 and just such a tug-of-war was going on between the soaring operation and one of the other airport tenants. Seems that this fellow didn't like the way them soaring types showed up for a week and acted like they owned the place. This combined with other frictions had caused the local office of the FAA to get involved. Our "friend" had complained that having automobiles on the airport was totally unsafe. Never mind that the contest had a ten-year history of safe operations, and that as beautiful as sailplanes are, they cannot taxi under their own power.

Gren Seibels was the contest manager. Gren could present a very diplomatic presence that did not reveal what he was really thinking. So with the FAA guys scheduled to come to the airport to determine whether the contest would be staged or not, Gren was our representative.

Gren and Ben Greene were in their best soaring togs, standing with the two coat-and-tied FAA officials looking out over the field. The conversation was serious, and all of us were holding our breath, hoping they'd come to some compromise and we'd be able to fly the race.

Suddenly, low over the trees, appeared a Maule. It looked as if it could be making an approach to the main runway. However, all the controls were crossed, the engine was being burped repeatedly, and the moves from near-stall to dive would have frightened anyone familiar with controlled flight. The Maule continued down the runway, and as

See Ya' at the Airport

it got to the far end did a rather steep climb-out, barely clearing the trees.

Mahlon had not seen the usual response from the gang down on the tiedown ramp. Thinking that he had surprised everyone, he decided to do an encore. Again, he approached the runway and began the same erratic flying. Much like the flying clown acts seen in airshows, Mahlon again thrilled the crowd. Confident now that all knew Mahlon had arrived, he lined up for the third time and did a landing that included squealing tires and flapping controls.

Mahlon often wore a mountaineer's hat that reminded you of the feud between the Hatfields and the McCoys. It had a wide brim all around and a cone on top shaped like the orange ones you see around highway construction sites. He taxied up to the old Bermuda High hangar, just a few feet from where the FAA boys were standing. The airport problems had suddenly become small potatoes — all the FAA wanted to do was talk to the guy with the big hat. Mahlon in his crazy way had actually saved the day. As he rode off in the black car with "For Official Use Only" stamped on the door, the race got underway and we didn't see any more officials of any kind for the rest of the week. Mahlon returned to us the next morning, saying nothing except that it had been "an interesting evening in Columbia."

Mahlon loved practical jokes. I got to see one of his favorites when we were towing trailers from Cordele, Georgia and stopped for gas. Sailplane trailers, being unusually long and low, always draw the question, "What you got in there?" That was Mahlon's cue. He'd tell how he traveled the country wrestling alligators in all kinds of shows; of the time he wrestled in Madison Square Garden before a crowd of 50,000 and the time he wrestled for President Eisenhower. He would tell his victim about "Ole Jake," the biggest and meanest of all 'gators: how strong Jake was with his 27-foot body, and that he had eaten three men and a horse. Mahlon would explain that Jake was asleep in that very trailer like a child on a long trip, and that we were headed back to Florida to let Jake go back to nature because he had grown too big for even Mahlon to wrestle.

I was amazed at how Mahlon could spin that yarn and have people actually believing him. Finally the inevitable question would come: "Can we see him?" At first Mahlon would tell them it's not safe, but

The Jokester

he'd move toward the trailer and as he talked would open the front hatch and peek in. Without fail, curiosity would overtake the victims — they just *had* to look. As they moved in, Mahlon would whisper a warning about not awakening the beast.

As they got very close and were peering to see the monster, Mahlon would reach down to the tongue of the trailer and mash a small hidden button. In one corner of the trailer he'd installed an old car starter with several pieces of rubber innertube attached to it. Suddenly, this loud flapping noise would come from the trailer as the rubber slapped the side. We heard screams, and streams of profanity. People would run all the way back into the station and warn everyone of the giant alligator that tried to bite them. One thing is for sure: Mahlon never tired of the set-up, and loved the reaction. I am certain that to this day there are folks around the country that still talk about the guy who wrestled alligators.

Mahlon had lots of tricks he loved to play on those who were actually in the contests. One of my all-time favorites was the "Chewin' Tabacca" routine. He'd see a crowd of pilots and crews gathered around the scoring shack in a circle, talking about the day's race. He'd wander up and start listening. Soon he'd reach in his back pocket and bring out a bag of Red Man chewing tobacco, open it up and take a big "chaw."

In a crowd that didn't tolerate smoking, the sight of Mahlon loading up would bring some raised eyebrows, and shuffling feet. Mahlon would continue to listen to the conversation as he really began to work that "chaw." Soon a rim of brown liquid would appear around his lips and with great ceremony he'd spit right in the middle of the circle. The silence could be heard all the way down the ramp. Mahlon would stand there with a puzzled look on his face, and finally say, "Does this bother you folks?" Some brave soul would say, "Why yes, Mahlon, that is a terrible habit." With that Mahlon would apologize over and over again and then without warning would swallow the entire brown mass in his mouth. This would bring startled looks and moans from the group, and usually break it up. Mahlon would walk away with a big grin on his face.

I watched him do this a dozen times, wondering how his stomach stood that wad of tobacco. One day we were sitting at a table in the office of Southwest Soaring down in Caddo Mills, Texas. Mahlon had laid his bag of Red Man on the table and I picked it up out of idle curiosity. I opened it, and noticed it looked different from the chewing tobacco I remembered from my misguided youth. I took a whiff, and it did not smell right either. Finally I took a pinch and tasted the stuff, expecting that acid taste to cover my mouth. Instead, it was raisins — all these years it had been raisins! Another of Mahlon's wonderful ruses.

Mahlon especially loved to dupe the ladies of soaring. His most-remembered stunt came during the World Championships in Hobbs, New Mexico, in 1983. Mahlon was a collector of soaring pins. He had pins from many of the contests he had been involved in, and pins he had traded with soaring types he had met over the years.

Pin trading at a World meet is a big deal, and everyone wears the pin of his team or country. Mahlon showed up at the championships with a rather large pin of the American flag which had a sailplane flying across the face of it. He wore this pin at the first official pilots' meeting. With the crews sitting in the back of the crowd, the conversation soon turned to Mahlon's pin. One of the well-known lady pin-traders approached Mahlon to see if she could trade him for that pin. Mahlon told her to meet him at his motel room about midnight and he would consider a trade; this statement was punctuated with a lecherous wink. Needless to say the reaction was not good. Mahlon did this for several days with as many women as he could, and soon had a reputation of being a dirty old man.

On the sixth day of the contest the crew section was abuzz with ladies pointing and whispering to each other. Just before the meeting, Mahlon had walked up to one of the young and well-built crews for the German team and offered her the pin with no strings attached. She had walked into the meeting proudly wearing that pin on her chest, displaying it to all the pin collectors. The smile on Mahlon's face reminded all of us of the Cheshire cat in Alice in Wonderland.

Not all of Mahlon's pranks ended in laughter. In 1978 the Standard Class Nationals were underway in Hutchinson, Kansas. The weather had been weak and on this day we stood down from flying. Mahlon was as bored as the rest of us. Hutch is a remote airfield and the entertainment possibilities left a lot to be desired.

The Jokester

Mahlon had heard that if you light an acetylene torch and then put out the flame, the unburned gas can be contained and will make a loud bang if struck with a sharp force. He started with milk jugs, filling them with acetylene, setting them some distance down one of the abandoned runways and shooting at them until they exploded. This was fun for a while, but didn't have the punch Mahlon was looking for.

Thinking that more gas would make a louder explosion, he set out to find the perfect container. In the old hangar he found a box of black plastic garbage bags — just what he was looking for. Along with another towpilot, Mahlon lit the torch then snuffed out the flame on the workbench. Now with the gas at perfect mix they began to fill the bag.

It was at this moment that one of the pilots in the contest walks into the shop and asks, "What are you doing?" Mahlon says, "We're making a bomb." With that the towpilot reaches down to unfold the bottom of the bag. The explosion is so loud that everyone on the airport hears it.

Along with several others I begin running toward the hangar. As we approach we see Chicho Estrada stagger out the door, and fall on the ground holding his ears. There are children screaming behind the hangar. As we enter we see the towpilot on the ground, writhing in agony. Mahlon is standing stunned in the middle of the place, saying over and over: "I screwed up, I screwed up."

The screams were coming from the McMaster kids who were playing in a sandbox behind the building. The concussion had blown the glass out of the windows and down on the kids; luckily they just sat where they were and wailed. The whole place had gone from a quiet day waiting for better weather to a holocaust that would go down in the annals of sailplane racing.

The kids were okay. The three guys went to the hospital. All had broken eardrums and Mahlon had first-degree burns on all exposed skin. The nurses had to use tweezers to pick the remains of the plastic bag out of his hide. He returned to the airport that afternoon and loaded up the Maule. Flying no higher than 500 feet because of the damage to his ears, he returned home to Florida to recover.

Mahlon was back at the next contest with a big grin. He knew he had messed up and admitted it to everyone. Soon he was back at his old tricks and a few new ones.

Mahlon was lost to soaring in a sailplane accident in Hobbs, New Mexico. To this day his legend continues to grow. Anytime a bunch of racing types go to dinner after a day of flying, the conversation sooner or later will drift to one of the Mahlon stories. Those of us who knew him get to laugh all over again, and those who did not get to hear about the greatest jokester in soaring.

RULES ON THE ROAD

In the past 33 years I have traveled a million miles in pursuit of competition soaring. The reason is simple: the most interesting and diverse people I could imagine are involved in this sport. The game is great to watch and sailplanes are sculptures suspended in air, but the main attraction has always been the personalities. Because we are in a game that is not putting money into anyone's pocket and the world is pretty much oblivious to what we are doing, we are free to experience all the emotions such a game can generate without cost in our daily lives. Among us is an important subgroup — one I have observed with great interest over the years and found to have endless ability to entertain and teach me.

I am not a parent. My approach to kids is different from those who practice the dark art called "parenthood." I am the luckiest of men in that children and young people will actually have something to do with me and not treat me as an "adult." This connection has always been a mystery to me, but I have enjoyed it ever since I can remember.

Rules on the Road

Over the years many of the young of all ages have climbed into my van and taken on both me and a summer of competition meets.

With puberty rolling over them like a Sherman tank and parents trying to steer them through this most awkward of times, the prospect of an escape from parental dictatorship via a soaring adventure has great appeal to a teenager. With a suitcase or two carefully packed by Mom with the proper number of folded clothes, including marked underwear, and a couple of hundred dollars in their pocket, they are ready for anything — or think they are. After last-minute instructions from a misty-eyed Mom and a silent hand-shake from Dad we load up into the van and soon are rolling down the highway for the start of our adventure.

I use several verbal games to gauge where we are in maturity. After an hour or so of driving in silence, my new friend decides to break the ice. Without fail, the first conversation goes like this: "What time is it?" to which I ask, "Do you have a watch?" "Yeah, but I never wear it." Then I ask, "Then why do you want to know what time it is?" Usually the answer is quite muted and accompanied by strained giggles: an answer only Captain Kirk and the Space Patrol could decipher. I do finally tell him what time it is, but explain I am not a 220-parrot who is going to chime in with the time whenever he demands it. I find a big shopping center at our next gas stop. Usually there's a Wal-mart or K-mart, and within a few minutes he has purchased an inexpensive digital watch. Problem solved, right? Well, maybe: I have seen the hardiest of watch batteries fade and die under the constant fiddling and button-pressing that only a teenager can give a new toy. Soon we are back to "What time is it?"

As the sun goes down it is time to find a motel room. I pull off the Interstate and into the first place that actually has the room price displayed. I tell my new friend to find something to do while I go into the office — and find out they are full for the night. I go back out expecting to see my new friend at shotgun, but he is not there. I take a quick look around and see him dive off the side of the pool with a huge splash. Not only do I not have a room — I do not have a place for a soaking wet teenager in my van. I tell him he will have to stand in the back on a towel while we drive around trying to find a room.

This is another lesson for me: be sure and tell them not to go into the pool until we actually have a room.

The Rules
The rules for traveling with Charlie are simple:
1. Be where I tell you to be, when I tell you to be there.
2. You are in charge of your own money.
3. You can only hang around with the kids at the meet.
4. Don't complain about my snoring.

Rule #1 covers working in the contest. The usual requirements are: Make the morning pilots' meeting, and be on time for the job you have chosen. For rule # 2, I suggest to the parents how much money the youngster will need during our time on the road. I keep half, and give the kid the other half as we start the trip. Rule #3 keeps the kid totally immersed in the competition.

What the kids wear, what time they go to bed, what they eat, when they bathe, and all the other things I have watched parents drive themselves crazy over, I just don't mention. This attitude has produced some interesting reactions. "Tonight, I am going to stay up all night!" is one I hear from time to time. "I am going to drink all the Pepsi I want" is another. This freedom they feel is a joy to watch. The truth is they are isolated by the location of most sailplane races, and they are under the influence of some of the best people I have ever met.

Consequences
I will admit that I do make them pay the price of not following the rules by letting them suffer the consequences. Driving through west Texas, I say, "Let's stop at a shopping center and pick up some groceries and magazines for the stay in the motel." At the store, I say, "Be back here in 30 minutes." We start checking things out together, but he finds something interesting and soon we are parted. I do the shopping, pick up some reading material, and head for the van. I check my watch and as the thirty minutes pass I crank up and drive off. I stay gone at least a half-hour, usually parking somewhere and reading the magazines I bought.

I return to the shopping center and without fail I am met before I can get parked. "Where did you go?" My answer is always the same: "You've got to be where you are supposed to be every time or you could get left." This usually shows I mean business, but not always. Another thing it does is show my friend that he really needs to know his home phone number and other information in case this was a real deal. I refuse to do what I have seen parents do for years: chase up and down aisles, or look into every store along the strip, just to remind this kid it's time to go.

If the problem persists I set up another "on time" situation. This time I make sure the lure is good: "After the finish gate closes today, let's you and me go see the new 'Star Wars' movie — meet me in front of the hangar at six." Several times I have looked in my rearview mirror to see a running kid with wildly flailing arms as I leave the airport right on time. Of course I don't go to the movie, and when I return to the airport my young friend is mad, and upset. I let it alone until the next day. When our work is finished, I say, "Why don't we try it again? Meet me at the hangar at six and we will make the show." As six rolls around I climb into the van, and there beside me is the kid. Soon I no longer have to worry about deadlines, and I never mention them again.

Money

Watching the way a young person handles rule #2 is most interesting. Handing a 14-year-old more money than he's used to is somewhat scary. Forbidden fruits come first: candy bars, soda pop, pinball machines and firecrackers are in the top ten during the first week. Money flows like water, with no thought that it will run out — after all, it never has before. The thing that floors me every time is: "You mean I have to *pay* for my meal?!" "Yes," I say, "who did you think was going to pay?" Soon hunger is playing havoc with the dream budget the kid has put together in his mind. Soon donut breakfasts and candy bar lunches are a thing of the past.

I begin to see the signs about four days before the next injection of cash is due. There are not so many candy bars around, and the kid was actually seen drinking water this morning. I begin to get questions on the cost of things, and the inevitable, "Can I get my money now?"

See Ya' at the Airport

The answer is always "No." Now real panic begins to set in. "What do you want me to do, starve?" is the whiney question I get. But he has made many friends at the contest, and knows when the moms are fixing lunch. I mention that I have seen him in a couple of mobile homes wolfing down baloney sandwiches at lunchtime, so I am not worried about his starving. I know times are really tough when we go through the cafeteria line and my friend gets a small box of cereal and small carton of milk. As we are sitting at the table he tells me this is not enough to eat and I get another request for the money early. I say, "Why don't you go out to the van and get those firecrackers you bought — maybe with a little milk and sugar they will fill you up." This remark does not go over well at all, and for the rest of the breakfast we eat in silence — or should I say, I eat in the silence.

As we are driving back to the airport I suggest finding some work at the field. "What kind of work?" I suggest checking with the pilots and see if anyone needs help putting on wings — by this time many wives have had enough of handling wings in the heat. I suggest he offer to put wings on for a dollar each. In most cases the kid will try this idea and within a day or two will have a route along the tie-downs, helping assemble gliders.

Finally the day comes when the second injection of money goes into their pocket. How things have changed! Gone is the spendthrift who blew money everywhere. Now we have the summer version of Scrooge. We are seeing money actually being saved, and we see a young person on a mission to make as much as possible before the race is over. On many occasions I have sent kids home with more money than they left with. To see this transformation is remarkable, and to watch a young person change so quickly is gratifying.

Bathing

Bathing is another area in which children have been coached since the earliest time. Mom not only schedules bathing but also dictates exactly how it will be done. I approach it from a different angle: I never mention bathing — I don't have time, I do a poor imitation of a parrot, and I don't want the responsibility. Now, I have to admit that a kid on the road away from parents can have some problem with bathing. I also must admit that an 11-year-old boy who has not bathed in a while has an odor that I can only describe as "kid funk." It is not the same odor as adults, but it does have the same power to repel. Several times I have come close to saying something, but so far, with time, the situation has taken care of itself. One example was a kid at Minden who had not washed the desert dust off in several days. He and a couple of other boys got bored during the lull between starts and finishes. Soon the teasing turned into a friendly wrestling match. As they were grabbing and tussling, suddenly everything came to a stop: "*You stink*" was shouted as the two boys ran away. My charge came over to me and casually asked, "Charlie, is there a shower here on the airport?" I gave him directions, and watched as he went off to the shower with his never-before-used bath towel.

This doesn't mean that all catch on. I was driving out of Hobbs, New Mexico, after a hard, hot contest with one of my kids at shotgun. He was looking out the window into the rear-view mirror. He turned to me and said, "Look, Charlie, my tan is coming off!" I looked over and saw what he was doing: rolling up the dirt that had stuck in the creases in his neck. "That's great, maybe you can put it in a box and save it for this winter." He looked at me with a very confused expression.

Sometimes, a motel swimming pool does the job. For girls, going swimming is a reason to take a bath, for boys swimming *is* a bath. I have learned over the years that any time the body is immersed in water is better than never.

At the Airfield

Rule #3 is the easiest to follow. As we travel I explain the basics of sailplane racing. I tell him who's hot, and who's not. I explain all the jobs: the gate, the launch, and weighing. I tell him to try them all, and pick what he wants to do. When we arrive at the airport, he is pretty quickly on his own as I go to work. Most of the kids who are at a contest have been there before, and they know not to waste time with shyness. Within hours new friendships have been formed, and as the contest goes on these friendships can grow into lasting relationships. My friend is swept into this circle of kids, and soon is talking about them as though they were lifelong buddies. This knot of kids only gets tighter as the contest days go by. They go to the pilots' meeting, not to hear the winner tell of his feats, but to group up and plan the day's activities. After the pilots' meeting and the assembly of sailplanes, there is a lag when there is no demand on their time. They stay on the airport, usually finding the coolest place to "hang out" while waiting for the first launch. They always find a game to play, be it hearts, gin rummy or something made up, and spend hours discussing the rules. They laugh and joke with each other; "one-upmanship" becomes the most important game.

The finish gate is the most popular job, and because it takes real teamwork the group must work out who will do what. I only explain that I want it done right, and lay out the basic system for getting sailplanes marked and finished in a national race. They always get it right after a little practice.

Romance is bound to break out in a group of teenagers. Watching the flirtations and games they play is interesting. It is both a sweet and repulsive ritual. They are so innocent and so naive that the dance is comical. Yet, it does remind you of your own youth, and how much worse you must have been. These romances become the subject of endless hours of gossip. Very seldom have I seen these infatuations go to the limit, but I can say that those involved learn a great deal about the other sex. A sailplane race has all the elements to create this result. Sun, long hours of freedom, no school, no jobs, and new friends are an elixir full of lifetime memories. Again I use one of my verbal soundings to judge where things might go. I admit it is a crude gauge but it does give me some idea of where we are in the chain of lightning known as puberty. It goes like this: "Which would you rather do; see a naked woman or set off a bomb?" The answer is usually black and white and gives me a rough idea of where we are. I did have one young man who was on the fence and took several minutes to answer the question. After much thought he turned to me and asked, "How big's the bomb?"

Taking kids on the road is a big responsibility. I have been through several emergencies with my kids: road rash from a fall on a bicycle; cuts from all manner of sharp objects, lost money, lost clothes, lost glasses, and lost cameras have all caused problems. I approached all these situations with the same philosophy: "They'll get over it." I am amazed at how resourceful and fast-thinking the young can be. Giving them the chance to run their own lives in this "confined freedom" is the best gift I can give them.

Learning

With me, the kids get the chance to learn without direction. They learn to do laundry, and how to separate the whites from the colors. They sharpen their social skills, they learn how to play team, and they learn a little about money. They get to make decisions about their appearance, without mom. Many learn to drive, as I make a point of letting them drive me around the airport during the day. They get to fly, if so inclined, and many pick up on the thrill of soaring during these summer adventures. They get to say anything they want, and ask any question that comes to mind. I treat them with respect, and am rewarded with questions and discussions I know they have not had before. I always give a straight answer. When you are not preaching, it is amazing how quickly you make friends.

I like it most when I get to take a kid to more than one contest. The best part is he is no longer a "rookie" — he is now the "old hand." They know the ropes, and they know the jokes. They get a chance to be leaders, or take on responsibility that is a challenge. I have seen them go from "bed-wetter" (a term used by the kids themselves to put down a whining friend) to National gate operator in a short period. No doubt the ages between 10 and 15 are a time of "wing trying." It is a delight to watch, especially if you are not a parent.

Looking Back

Over the years there have been many, and like an old schoolteacher I cannot remember all the kids I've had around me. What is fun at fourteen is not even in the picture by nineteen. They are moving at lightning speed toward adulthood, and independence. Having been in sailplane racing for over thirty years, I get a chance to look back from time to time. Usually it happens during the course of a race day. In front of me is a face I recognize, but it is different and distant. After a couple of sentences I realize this is a person who was at a contest or two with me sometime in the past. Finally, when they see that I know who they are, I will hug them and start asking questions. Are you out of college? Where are you living? The questions wind down until we start talking about the races and the time he traveled with me. It is then that I realize that the summer trip was a real memory for this kid.

I hope to be able to give kids in soaring this racing adventure for as long as possible. The real truth is, I'm the one who is having the best adventure: being with the young will make you young. Sailplane racing has many attractions for me. The greatest of these is a day on the road with a kid.

KIDNEY FAILURE

I was never one for doctors. Of course I was going to live forever and had no reason to waste time with medical check-ups and doctor visits. That was my outlook well into my forties. As this story shows, I have since more than made up for that dumb assumption.

I returned to work at the auto shop in September of '91. After a full day of repairing cars I found I was exhausted. My sister took the bull by the horns and scheduled a doctor's appointment for me. I went reluctantly – I remembered some of the things these guys did from my Navy days: They seemed to think nothing of going into orifices that were designed for one-way traffic – the wrong way. Needles, sticks, wooden paddles jammed down my throat, and a "turn and cough" procedure convinced me that if I escaped the torture I'd never again willingly walk through a door with "MD" on it. (That thought is now a long-lost idiot dream.)

A couple of days later I got a call to return to the office for a "consultation" which I of course interpreted as a way to get more

Kidney Failure

money – after all, I was a healthy, strapping, 220-pound, 50-year-old man. The doctor told me in blunt terms that I had "end stage renal disease." He went on to explain that my unchecked high blood pressure had damaged my kidneys to the point that I had less than 25% capacity left. I immediately retreated to every patient's first line of defense: denial. I remember stepping into the elevator saying to myself, "He doesn't know what the hell he is talking about – I feel great." I was soon to learn he knew exactly what he was talking about and that this disease would change my life forever.

The kidneys continued to fail through the winter of 1992-93. I went to the SSA Convention in Chicago where I had my last visit with Johann Kuhn. Johann was very sick, but we sat in the hall after a presentation and talked and had a few laughs. I left that convention driving south with a feeling of sadness. My ankles were swollen to the point I'd have to stop every couple of hours and get into the van bed with my feet up. When I got home I gave up denial – mainly because it was not working – and decided to go for being mad. There's nowhere useful to direct being mad except at yourself, and no renal patient worth his salt is ever going to do that. The medical industry must be the culprit and becomes the target. I felt I was not getting the answers I needed and that the doctors were uncaring.

I was so sick by the time the 1993 Chester regional contest came around that I thought I might not make it. I went to the meet as the gate and the CD. I found that I could overcome the fatigue long enough in the morning to get the task designed and hold a good pilots meeting. I'd rest in the van until launch time, drifting in and out of sleep. At the gate, I'd lay down until the first sailplane would call the IP, then get into position and work the start until it was over. Back into the van and to sleep until someone would call, "2 miles out" then into the gate chair as the first finisher crossed the line. I got through that contest with the help of all my gate buddies but knew I'd never make it through the season ahead of me.

I was so mad about my condition that I went so far as to start ambushing doctors. While in the hospital for yet another battery of tests, I noticed that the head of the transplant group was giving a medical symposium at a local hotel. I got dressed up in a coat and tie and snuck into this. The doctor's name was Dan Hayes; when he got through talking about stuff that made no sense to me, I raised my hand and asked a question. He answered it with a strange look on his face. I asked another and his response was "You are not a doctor, are you?" "No," I said, "I'm one of your patients!" Dr. Hayes told me that if I'd be quiet he'd talk with me after the symposium. I agreed and sat through another hour of medical discussions I had no clue about.

Dr. Hayes came to me after shaking hands with folks as they left and said to follow him to the parking lot. I thought he was going to give me a few words then get in his car and drive away. Instead, he leaned against the front of my van and for almost two hours he listened and talked. Dr. Hayes did more for me that night than anyone had since I'd entered the world of renal failure. He took my badgering and griping in stride and when I had exhausted every insult I could think of he began to talk. What he said was that I was in a bad situation and that the medical industry was never going to cure me. It could prolong my life and give me relief from the pain I was feeling but I would have to accept the facts and deal with them in a responsible way if I wanted to live.

I went home that night and thought long and hard about my situation. I was finally getting to where I wanted to be in competition soaring. I'd have to face this problem and solve it the best way I could if I was going to stay where I'd worked hard to get. I changed my attitude completely. I began to study everything I could find on renal failure. Lynn Greenblatt was working at Johns Hopkins, and she was a gate buddy. She sent me reams of information on renal failure. I spent hours poring over the pages and bought a medical dictionary. I discovered that the medical industry has its own language – a 13-letter word can simply mean, "You have gas."

Once I broke this language down into something I could understand, I learned fast. I could now talk sensibly to doctors and I began to realize they appreciated a patient that took interest in his own problem. I was breaking down that invisible wall that always exists between doctor and patient. I learned not to complain but to explain what I was feeling. When not face to face with my doctors, I would simply write a letter and mail it. This system still works today. I took *Soaring* magazine with me to appointments to show them something about my life. I was trying to get my head above the crowd and it was working.

It was two weeks after the '94 Chester regional when I could no longer tolerate the poisons the kidneys could not remove. I went into the hospital to have a tube put into my peritoneal cavity, which would allow me to do peritoneal dialysis. Because I wanted as much independence as possible I was given the option of doing this dialysis "manually." The system was simple: Four times a day, I hooked myself up to a two-bag system. One bag started out empty and drained fluid from my peritoneal cavity; the other contained fresh fluid to refill it. This "jiffy-lube" procedure carried off enough of the poisons to give me a life. I was up and running on this system before my first scheduled contest at Mifflin. The doctors were reluctant to approve me going out on the road so soon after starting, but did not stop me.

There were problems to deal with. Every thirty days I got a shipment of dialysis fluids, tubes and bags. I had to put some 800 pounds of supplies in my van before I left home and make arrangements for the next three shipments to meet me on the road. I was stopped twice in the first month by the highway patrol checking to see what I was carrying (a van with overloaded springs is always suspect).

I found that peritoneal dialysis fit in perfectly with a contest day: I did one exchange in the morning before the pilots meeting – I'd rig up a nail in the wall of the office I was using and hang the bags there. I could work on the weather and the previous day scoring and do an exchange at the same time. I had the van set up so that I could sit in the driver's seat with a bag hung from one of the braces in the roof. Before the launch I'd hook up and drive where I needed to be while doing another exchange. The time between the starts and finishes could also be used, but usually I'd get hooked up right before the first finishes and do an exchange as sailplanes whistled across the finish line. One more before hitting the sack and I was done for the day.

When on the road, I'd stop and get hooked up, then drive until the exchange was complete – it slowed the traveling but did not stop it. I learned some tricks: Putting two liters of cold fluid into your belly could be pretty uncomfortable. I put the bags on the dash and let the

See Ya' at the Airport

sun warm them. I also built a tray and a switch on the heater system so I could heat the bags on the passenger side of the van after dark.

Getting rid of the used fluid presented a problem at first. The instructions stated that the bag should be emptied into a toilet. I have to admit I seldom use a toilet in the course of a contest day and discarded this instruction immediately. For a while I stabbed them with a pocketknife, but waiting for the fluid to drain was tiresome. I decided to see if I could "bust" them by swinging them over my head and slamming them on the ground. It worked. I told my doctors about this technique and they were intrigued. One morning I met three doctors in the parking lot of the kidney clinic and, having saved several bags, I slammed them one by one on the pavement. They were both amused and appalled at my disposal system. All agreed it was very quick, but they had no plans of letting me show it to other patients.

Because I made the system work for me, I was able to travel to competitions all during the time I was on dialysis – and on the waiting list for a kidney. I finally got a kidney transplant in March of '95. The transplant operation was fairly simple compared to other surgeries (they put the new kidney in your abdominal cavity, where there's plenty of room), but recovering from it was not. I was in the hospital for two weeks while the kidney slowly improved my health. Two weeks in the hospital is like being sentenced to 30 years in prison, but it was the only way for me to get better. I was tortured by several things, the worst of which was a device called a "Folly" – a tube placed in the bladder to keep things flowing. I won't go into detail except to say it was a great relief to get rid of it.

The difference between dialysis and the transplanted kidney was huge. I was no longer a "zombie." I felt good and felt my life returning, as I was able to do more and more. I returned to soaring competitions, and began working again.

All went well until the contest in Uvalde in 2001. I got the old man's problem of enlarged prostate and this put a strain on the kidney. I went down with a kidney infection that winter that put me in the hospital again. Back to my old friend "Folly" and other indignities as the doctors tried to save the transplant. They did prolong it, but in May 2004 while at the nationals in Mifflin the kidney finally failed.

Kidney Failure

I spent eight days in the hospital as the doctors and nurses worked to get me back to some level of independent life. I went into surgery where three separate operations were done. The most important was to put in another peritoneal dialysis tube – I was back on the "jiffy-lube" system. I was able to return to soaring later in the season and worked a regional and two Nationals.

I admit that this has been a real trial for me. But I have found humor in this situation. I have come to love telling off-color jokes to doctors and nurses. Nurses seem to like the jokes – especially if they are dirty. They live with death and tragedy every day and if you can make them laugh they will remember you. They also will remember you if you play tricks on them. My favorite is to go into the little waiting room and take off all my clothes. I am supposed to put on a gown but it hides little and never closes in the back. I love to see the expression on their faces when they walk in and there before them is a naked short fat guy – it surprises them every time!

During my last hospital stay I received a large and beautiful flower arrangement from the contestants and staff at Mifflin. Every nurse who came into my room commented on this magnificent array of roses of all colors. I was on hemo-dialysis each day and watched the nurses in that unit work very hard to give some very sick folks some quality of life. My escort showed up one morning and I got an idea. I put this big beautiful arrangement on my chest as they rolled me into the dialysis unit. I gave every nurse a rose and put the rest on the main desk. From this point on I was the hit of the unit; I was treated like a celebrity and everyone knew my name.

Though it may sound strange, I have been lucky throughout my kidney failure. I have never met a doctor or nurse who did not have my best interest at heart. At times it has been a rough ride but at times it has opened people to me and I have felt comforted and supported.

No one knows what the future holds. As I write this, there seems to be a chance of another kidney transplant in a couple of months: another operation, another hospital stay, another chance of a period of life a little closer to normal. When you don't know what the future will be like, I guess it's smart to make the most of the present.

HALL OF FAME

In 1993, Rudy Opitz and Charlie Spratt were inducted into the United States Soaring Hall of Fame. The induction ceremony took place at the National Soaring Museum (NSM) in early 1994. The following article by William Gallagher appeared in Volume 16.2.1994 of the NSM Historic Journal.

Calling Charlie Spratt the nation's most sought-after soaring competition director, distance record-holder and U.S. Team Member Karl Striedieck (Hall of Fame, 1980) told Hall of Fame banqueters that the 1993 inductee had worked at 198 regional contests, two Nationals and two World Championships.

Spratt has served as director of 79 of the Regionals and 28 of the Nationals – "Which means that he's the boss and has the responsibility for the conduct of these competitions." Striedieck said.

Cataloguing Spratt's accomplishments, Striedieck added that Spratt has published 110 newsletters and written several articles for *Soaring* magazine.

Hall of Fame

"I've been a 'Charlie watcher' since about 1974 when I first met him in Chester," Striedieck said. He added that it has been said that Charlie's career started around 1969 when he just wandered down to the airport, became an airport junkie "like the rest of us," ending up at a Chester and getting involved in sailplane competition. Striedieck said that he was able to see Charlie evolve from the kind of person who just 'showed up' at soaring events, to the person who is the nation's most sought-after competition director. Internationally, his reputation as a contest director is well-known and respected.

"During his successful climb, Charlie has conquered a lot of obstacles," Striedieck said, then added, "No, not conquered, because if you conquer, someone gets defeated and Charlie does not defeat people. He wins." The speaker said that Charlie attains his objectives in such a way that everybody comes out a winner. It's one of his strongest points. "He's made some big sacrifices in his personal life, in his relationships and of course, financially, to make the sport a whole lot better," Striedieck said.

He said that there were dozens of kids, and maybe one or two in this audience, who aren't kids anymore, who remember how Charlie touched their lives. One of those was Dirk Elber (Newport News, VA) who wrote a poem in praise of Charlie. "I'd like to read it to you, Striedieck said. "It's better than I could say."

Charlie
Who is this man with the common name?
To the soaring community there is only one Charlie
What is he...the best competition pilot?
Hardly
The top meteorologist?
No, but he does know the weather
No, this red-headed Carolinian is known near and far as the best at his job
He controls the doors to the contest path
Diligence, patience and iron rules;
That's how he deals with the contest world
Warmhearted, and a quick joke;

That's how he deals with the rest of the world
But his work aside, it is his cohorts that bring him respect of the many airport parents
He finds the airport brats; spoiled kids of pilots
In an hour he has trained them to use their youth for the good of the sport
The gate is full of kids and their coke bottle binoculars, scanning the skies
Fast legs, Charlie calls and has an errand for us
This is Charlie's way of running the best organized gate in the world
For his work, a full-time volunteer job, the home of the soaring community welcomes this man
From the view from one of his brats, I say,
"Thanks for the experiences; for they are ones I will not soon forget."
So, for that I say, "Charlie Spratt, good thanks..."

Striedieck concluded by saying that when we're all retired or up in cloud heaven, we'll be reminiscing about all the great people we've known in soaring. "The person that we're going to remember the very longest because he's touched more that the mechanical part of our lives is this guy right here… Charlie Spratt," he said amid cheers and a room-shaking ovation.

Spratt opened by saying that he was honored to be here along with Rudy Opitz, one of his childhood heroes. He allowed that he has set a world record today in that he had worn a coat and tie longer than he ever had in his life. He continued, "I have a hard time talking about soaring with a tie on." Then, grabbing a duck-bill cap and clamping it over his carrot top, he added, to cheers from the audience, "I can hardly talk about it without wearing a ball cap either."

Spratt said that this was truly a great occasion for him. He was very excited about it so he asked friends what he should do and received many suggestions.

"The one that I took up on, "he said, was, 'What Soaring Has Meant To Me.' I want to read it to you, because I want to make sure that I get it all in there.

"Soaring is waking up, looking out of my old van and knowing

Hall of Fame

that we will race today, looking down an empty ramp with dew glistening off the wings of sailplanes at rest, the quiet breakfast in the camping area with small talk and the smell of coffee. Soaring is the conversational hum that always precedes a pilots meeting – intense and yet comforting – these meetings squeeze the glue that holds us all together. The winners talk, always with confidence; the lauchmaster's stern look as he describes 'the way it will be', the endless search for the perfect ballast system; and the endless waiting at the water for a turn to fill and heave those heavy water bags.

"Soaring is the grid shuffle where man and machine melt into a geometric form that has been the subject of a thousand photos; the sound of the first tug's crank-up; and the building excitement as each engine fires. Like magic, the gaggles form and soon the sky is filled with a dance that has inspired me since the first time I saw it. Soaring is the tension the first call to the gate brings on, the rush of excitement as the leaders call IP; the sound of a sailplane at speed, from on high a whisper that becomes a roar as the planes hit the mark time and time again; the moment of peace when it is clear they are all on course.

"Soaring is the quiet time between the starts and the finish when all of us who support the racers sit and wait. Soaring is the snap to attention that can only come from the first 'two minutes out' call – searching the horizon for that little white slit in the blue - suddenly seeing the smoke of ballast release and hearing the ever called ' I see him'. Soaring is the sound of a sailplane at redline as it crosses the finish line, a sound that chirps like no other on the face of the earth. The release I feel as I say the words 'good finish', the wave from the cockpit, and the cool slap of ballast as it sprays across the gate are true marks on my life. Soaring is the wait for that last pilot to cross the finish line long after all the others. Soaring is the grace of the landing, the sound of the whoop as pilots open the canopies after a good day, hearing the war stories as the crews wash the wings and rip the tape, the gathering at the turn-in, the intense search for their names on the score sheets, and the hands in the air explaining every turn and every thermal. Soaring is the smile on the winner's face and the disappointment in the eyes of the losers. Soaring is the true feeling of family as we gather at some watering hole, eating and talking about all the things that bond us. Soaring is watching the sun go down on the ramp with a beer in one hand and a set of liar's dice in the other, the laughs you get from corny jokes and the pleasure of being among your own. Soaring is lying down with the breeze blowing through, seeing a clear sky full of stars and knowing that tomorrow will bring another day of what you love best.

"I traveled the world, as though a millionaire, stopping where I wanted and doing what I wanted. I have stood on the ancient wrinkles of the Appalachians, and watched my friends roar by at speed, and I have stood on the desert floor and stared into the blue for that little white spot climbing in the wave. I have heard the thunder over the Whites, and the thunder in the winner's heart. I have seen the storms over Hutch, and felt the heat of Cordele. I have seen the water freeze in the dump valves at Chester, and sailplanes launched as the snow was flying at 'The ridge'. I have seen the mark reach 110 on the ramp at Marfa and the rain gauge overflow at Ionia. I have smelled the oil fields of Hobbs and felt the humidity of Winterhaven. I have stood in the open at Uvalde and enjoyed the shade of Sugarbush. I have roamed through every state in the union, in every season. I have adventured in exotic places like New Zealand, South Africa, Europe and South America, all because of my love for this sport. It has been an amazing junket and a gift I will never forget.

"Nothing will ever compare to the people. For me, for all these years it has been the people of Soaring that have kept me close. I grew up soaring. I matured soaring – well maybe not completely! I have stood in a circle of champions and been accepted. I have seen the new ones with their hope and aspirations on their sleeves. I have seen them grow and I have seen them go. I have seen the test of character a thousand times and I have seen those who passed and those who failed. Each race is a play and everyone has a part – the champion, the vanquished, the supporters and the supported, the cheerleader and the antagonist – with cumulus clouds for a stage and runways for props. I am the most fortunate of all because I was a part of it all.

"The women – Oh, the women. Women windblown, women without makeup and without fashion, and yet more beautiful than any model in any magazine. True women, intelligent women who have shown me all facets of the opposite sex. Women who have been real friends and have shared their feelings with me. I have seen them

Hall of Fame

Grabbing a duck-bill cap and clamping it on his carrot top, he added, "I can hardly talk about soaring without wearing a ball cap - no one would recognize me."

Top Row, L to R: Howie Burr, Bill Schweizer, Karl Striedieck, Ernie Schweizer, Bernald Smith.
Middle Row: Hal Lattimore, Al Santilli, Floyd Sweet, Ted Sharp, Paul A. Schweizer.
Bottom Row: Charlie Spratt, Rudy Opitz, Virginia Schweizer

enjoy the fact that their mate's joy is soaring and have supported this endeavor without understanding the joy themselves. I have spent time with many and touched a precious few. I have flirted and romanced with Soaring as the wine. Holding hands on long walks down darkened runways or embracing under a wing – the passion all the stronger because of Soaring. Although none of these encounters has led to a permanent bond, I continue to seek that one that will love me and give me the freedom to chase my dreams in Soaring.

"I have been fired in controversy and quenched in acceptance. I have wandered through the politics of Soaring and moved from an outsider into the very center of the beast. I have created powerful enemies and even more powerful allies. I have won battles and lost wars, used compromise and gained insight. I have been a leader and I have been led. I've made poor decisions and at times appeared to be a genius. I have agonized over rules and been glad I had them to fall back on. I have felt the sting of real mistakes and the pleasure of a job well done. Soaring has given me the chance to use my brain and personality in a most unique way.

"When the final account is called, I will stand at some gate on some airport with the realization that I have lived an amazing life, as I am living it now. No amount of money or power could give me what Soaring has laid before me. I could not imagine a greater adventure for myself. I have cussed, cried, danced, laughed and done it all on the silent white wings of Soaring. I have never pursued money or material things – they only slow me down – but when the time comes to count it up, I will be a multimillionaire, not in dollars, but in experience, memories and best of all, Friends. Soaring has given me all of this and I will forever be truly thankful for this wonderful gift."...

Ever the pixie, Spratt proceeded to describe the workings of the 'Oh-oh Squad.' He related the precipitating incident that led to the deployment of the 'Oh-oh Squad'. In the haste of pregrid maneuvering, a 4 WD vehicle inadvertently backs over two feet of sailplane wing…'Oh-oh,' the squad is immediately activated. 'Anybody can be a member,' he said. All you do is come on over to wherever the catastrophe is happening and begin to say, 'Oh-oh'. You have to point at things and you have to lift up things, and every once in a while you have to whisper a little bit, 'Oh-oh.'

Hall of Fame

He closed by saying, 'What I've said here tonight, I truly feel about soaring. I love the sport. I've been in it for 28 years, been all over the world and have had a wonderful time. It's the people that keep me in it, the children especially. I hope to be in it for a long time to come. I'm truly honored to be asked to be in the United States Soaring Hall of Fame. Thank you very much.

THE TUBE

This story has little to do with soaring except that during all those years I moved from contest to contest, I worked in a car repair shop in the winter to support my addiction to traveling and soaring meets.

Like all true independent shops we worked on anything that came to the door and many that were towed to the lot. To be able to work on a Ford one minute and a BMW the next takes a lot of experience and a lot of knowledge of the basics of all automotive systems.

I worked off and on in this one shop for 25 years. The owner and I were friends as long as I was putting repaired cars out the door. All shops are the same: your rank in the pecking order depends entirely on the size of your pay check at the end of the week. Of course it was all male in the repair bays – the only female sat at a desk in the front office in a clean dress.

In this all-male realm practical jokes and "one-upmanship" were endless. From throwing a loaded condenser on a work bench, to loosening the clamp on someone's air wrench hose, to stuffing shop rags up an exhaust pipe, all the tricks were done and they all were fun. This was especially true when a new guy showed up. They would come straight from the vocational college and my boss gave most of them a chance. For us old hands it was fresh meat. We got two 15-

The Tube

minute breaks each day and a 30-minute lunch. The minute that kid went on his first break the set-ups began. We especially loved the guys who were prone to brag about how good a mechanic they were. With a sneaky removal of a rotor button we could change a routine spark plug replacement into an all day laugh-a-thon complete with suggestions that had him trying to look down the gas tank pipe with a flashlight.

The shop was located about a mile off the end of Runway 27 in Charlotte, NC. When the wind was right commercial jet after jet would pass over us, whining low and dirty. It was loud but all of us were used to it and thought nothing of it – except when we had a new guy.

An air compressor fed all the work benches in the shop and it had to be hefty to handle a fully working shop. It was located out behind the shop and you could hear its muffled pumping from time to time. The trick was simple: all it took was an old innertube and a piece of air hose. The compressor had a bleed valve on it and with a couple of small clamps the tube could be hooked directly to the valve. Open the valve wide open and get a quick result or let it fill slowly and the culprit could be working at his station for some time before the "BIG BANG."

When an innertube is blown up to destruction the result is not so much a loud pop but more of a thump and with that much air release it can put out a pretty good concussion wave. This is especially true when it's leaning against the side of the compressor house.

With everyone working hard trying to get work out the door the explosion makes even the culprit jump. The old hands know immediately what has happened. Among lots of four-letter expletives someone shouts "plane crash" and we all run out of the shop to find the site. Unknown to our victim, there is a long-abandoned aircraft wrecking yard in the ravine behind the shop. A crumpled set of Luscombe wings and the wadded-up frame of an old Cessna 150 lay among the weeds. As we come over the rise we gasp and point. We send the kid down to find the body while we go for help. Of course all we did was go back to work and leave him down in that ravine searching. Soon he comes back and suffers the jibes of the crew including "What did you find?" and then "Maybe they walked away".

See Ya' at the Airport

This trick ended forever the day someone (we will never know who) hooked a giant truck tube to the valve. I will never forget the shouts of "holy s---, and what the f---! as the boss drove to the back of the shop with a customer's car. The tube was huge – it was more than half way up the side of the shop and was the most dangerous thing I have ever seen. Even so we all wanted to hear it blow – the boss included. Of course none of us wanted to get close to it, much less try to shut off the compressor.

The solution was to shoot it. The only weapon in the shop was a crossbow one of the guys had gotten in a trade. He had never shot it and did not know how to load it. By now the race shop across from us had seen the commotion and we were beginning to attract spectators. When two UPS trucks stopped I knew things were getting out of hand quickly. With lots of "Here, let me do it" from several of the guys the bow is finally loaded. The boss is going to do the shooting. We are at least one hundred yards back when he pulls the trigger. The arrow hits the mark and there is a huge deep "WHUMP" as the tube explodes in a cloud of dust. We are all slammed by the concussion and as things settle we look around for any damage. The only thing that happened was Willie's hat had been blown off and for all of us it was the first time in the fourteen years he had been in the shop we had seen him bare-headed. The boss turned to all of us and said "That trick is over and if I find out who did it he'll work for half commission for a week."

Walking back into the shop someone mumbled "Willie, I never knew you were bald." Then it started: "Well I think Bert did it", with the retort "He ain't smart enough." It went on for weeks and we were a neighborhood attraction for a while as the story and the tube got bigger.

Working in a car shop is good work if you don't mind an explosive joke every now and again.

Charlie Spratt's Sailplane Racing News

October 2, 1984

WEAK BUT WONDERFUL AT NEW CASTLE

Hi Race Fans,

Karl Striedieck out of Port Matilda, PA flying a borrowed AS-W 20 flew to his fourth regional win this season at New Castle, Virginia. Robbie Robertson in his well-prepared Ventus A flew to a strong second-place win with a gain of 80 points on the last day. The 15m class was well-represented with 15 entries.

In the standard class Ted Falk in his standard Libelle flew a very steady race to win over the likes of Ed Byars and Tonk Mills. The standard class had a wide variety of ships including the standard Cirrus, Pegase, AS-W 19. Libelle, and the LS-4.

The auxiliary-powered sailplane class had four entries and were using the Don Pollard scoring system (more on this in the second section). Dave Stevenson took the class with an impressive 400-minute win over Bob Tawse.

John Seymour did a fantastic job as Contest Director; so well in fact that it led Ed Byars to make the following comment: "Never has one gotten so much out of so little." The weather this year was not the usual front passage with the accompanying ridge lift. Instead it was hazy with weak thermals. On the best weather day, which was the second contest day, the C.D. called the P.O.S.T. task and Striedieck gained 200 points by flying 233 miles! We got four contest days out of the advertised six, and all the contestants said it was a challenging and interesting race.

The Blue Ridge Soaring Society did a great job of putting on this race, and I cannot tell you how beautiful of a soaring site New Castle is. You must see it for yourself to really appreciate it. This is the last race of the season and New Castle couldn't be a better place to finish it.

I'm looking forward to next season. It should be a great one. Till then,

See you at the airport.

Charlie

"Mark"

New Castle scores, pp. 11-14

SAILPLANE RACING NEWS

October 2, 1998

Hi Race Fans,

I started SRN in 1980. It was a one-page sheet with the final scores on one side and some of the big events on the other. I would go to the nearest copy shop and have as many copies as I needed made. Then I would address envelopes by hand, lick stamps and put them into a mailbox.

As the popularity of Sailplane Racing News grew, I began to have trouble with the volume of stuff I had to do while traveling between meets. Just when I thought I was going to have to give it up, Carson Gilmer came to my rescue. Carson had a company that handled lots of mailings, and he made arrangements to keep it alive until I could solve the problems of getting it into so many hands.

Janice Hoke and I have been friends since the "good ole days" down in Chester, S.C. Janice has a degree in French and was working at home putting out several newsletters in the Reno area. It was an agreement made in heaven. Janice has a real interest in soaring. Mike

Sailplane Racing News

Hoke has been in soaring longer than I have, and he inspired Janice to fly. They fly out of Air Sailing.

Janice and Mike have twin boys (men now) who have traveled the country with me working gates and crewing. Charlie and Bryan run a better gate than I ever thought of. The best part is that both these guys have taken up soaring in a big way. You will see both their names on score sheets and record books in the near future. With this kind of support, Sailplane Racing News grew and grew.

The best years were the mid 1980's and the early '90's. We had lots of subscriptions, and we were the place to get the latest and hottest news. Both Janice and I enjoyed chasing the news and reporting on the races. Janice is a master of putting things together, and her ability to make me look like I know how to spell and write have always amazed me. We did flash issues and late-breaking stories, and truly enjoyed being the lightning rod for all the latest.

A new dawn broke when the first PC's came on the scene. When the Internet got up and running, we began to see a drop in interest and subscriptions. Janice and I agreed that we would not chase the new system; instead, we would try to find points of interest that would not be found on the Web. For awhile this worked for us, and our subscriptions stayed even. Janice and I also agreed that we would not raise our price and instead cut an issue when the cost of production cut into our share of the profits. As time went on, we went from eight issues a season down to four. Last year it was down to three.

Both Janice and I knew that someday it would come to an end, but kept going out of loyalty to those who stayed with us from the start. Early this year, I was approached by the SSA to put Sailplane Racing News on the SSA Web page. It was a good offer and a chance for me to continue to write about sailplane racing. The saddest part for me was the fact that this would mean the end of this wonderful working relationship I have with Janice.

The speed at which it is necessary to get the news out precludes any of the editorial work that Janice did. I know there is a spell checker on my computer, but nothing will ever replace the work Janice did to make me look and sound good.

What this means is that you are reading the last printed issue of Sailplane Racing News. It has been a large part of my life. It gave me

See Ya' at the Airport

a platform in times when I thought I needed it. It has been, and I hope will continue to be, a great way to keep the racing community informed on what is happening at events they could not attend.

The best part has been the ability to spread good news about the people that make up the racing community. I have reported hundreds of births and sadly, many deaths. I have written jokes I knew would make people laugh and have written things that made them sad. It has been a wonderful run, but time and invention march on, and Sailplane Racing News is a victim of that march.

I hope you will join me in the new computer age. I hope you will join me as I do my best to put you at the race and talk about the people who are there. Most of all I hope that I can report the races for years to come because it has become such a part of me.

See you on the Web!
Charlie

June 22, 1984

SAILPLANE RACING HISTORY

When was water ballast first used in American competition? In talking with Don Pollard, he thinks it was 1947 at the Wichita Falls KS Nationals. A fellow by the name of Richard (Dick) Comey made a free distance flight of over 300 miles from there to Tucumcari NM to put himself in the lead which he never relinquished. He flew with 25 gallons of water which gave him penetration the others didn't have. His ship was factory-built with the ballast system.

Who built the ship? you ask. None other than the Schweizer brothers. It was an all-metal Schweizer 1-21 of which only two were built. So next time you're ballasting up and the hose breaks, or you strain your back lifting those water jugs, remember ole Paul and Ernie, they started it all!!

Sailplane Racing News

July 16, 1984

NEW STATUS SYMBOL

Being weighed on the grid at Ephrata became a status symbol, as the top ten were weighed every day. After Minden and now Ephrata, weighing has become low profile with a minimum of penalties.

December 11, 1984

CHRISTMAS WISH

It comes but once a year in all its glory,
This time that's filled with the Christmas story.

But give to me this summer past,
With ships on the grid, and daylight that lasts,
A gate popping with the start of the race,
And rewards for those who set the pace,
Towplanes roaring overhead
Coming home when the sun is red.

Give me the friends who race the white wings.
Give me the summer when no sleigh bell rings.
Christmas is a beautiful time of year,
But it's the silent race I long to hear.

See you at the airport.
Charlie

See Ya' at the Airport

May 7, 1985

IT WAS GOOD WHILE IT LASTED: CHESTER

Hi Race Fans,

Never in the 17 year history of Chester regionals have we had it so good. The practice day and the first race day were the "best." Soaring to 9.500 AGL and blasting around a 230 mile task at 82 mph led Robbie Robertson to say, "This is like Hobbs!!" Eric Mozer flew the new Discus to a first-day win in the Standard Class. Pretty impressive with guys like Striedieck, Byrd, Byars and Jacobs "chasin' him."

The mother lode high that brought the great practice day and first race day weather was showing its age by the second race day, and we saw slower speeds at the finish. Striedieck "blew them away" by finishing 4 mph faster than everybody. Sam Giltner pulled within 50 points of Robertson, and Eric dropped to second, "but not by much."

By the way this was a blue day.

The third day shut down fast, with lots of "clag" early and a 94 mile task was called. This was the famous "blue day survival test" with Al Buzzard and Johnny Byrd really "hangin' in there." The weather went into the tank as the front passed, and after two race days and a torture test, most welcomed a rest day.

Fourth race day was blue from start to finish. If you were a sunbather this was your day, if you were a racer you were in trouble. C.D. Seibels and his own chosen pilots' committee of Striedieck (Cat.1) and Sam Giltner (local hotshot) along with weather man Harry Senn decided to gamble on a long task due to the fact that the Chester area has been under a drought for three months. Also, there was no water on the ground from the passing storms.

However it was not to be, as a northwest wind developed, bringing wave from the Smokeys and destroying the lift. We ended up with a distance day, and it was scored on a thousand points. Alfonso Jurado led the 15 meter class, and the two Std. Class leaders got 1000 pts. each. The land-outs torpedoed the scheduled banquet. I feel bad for the folks who put in on (Bermuda High) but for me it was one of the best I've ever been to. It was sort of a "all you could eat" affair. Eight of us showed up, and two of them were "puny."

The last contest day was a Chester Classic, except for the same old problem of "no Cu's." A hundred and fifty-six miler was called, with all but one pilot having a speed finish. Ed Byars and Al Buzzard led their classes with last-day wins (These guys never get to tell their stories.).

Chester gave us our first chance to see the new Discus in action and gave Gren and Trudy Seibels a great race with which to end 17 years of contest organizing. Chester got the season under way with a "boomer."

See you at the airport.
Charlie

May 7, 1985

FUNNIES

The Academy Awards of Soaring were held at Chester this year and to give you an idea of the caliber of these awards, Andy McQuigg won the academy award for being the lowest profile pilot at the meet (he didn't show up!).

John Seymour won a special award of excellence in combat conditions for not only being an excellent "Pee" bomber, but for his ingenious way of disguising the bombs as apple juice by putting an apple core in each bag.

May 21, 1985

AN ACCIDENT AT WINTER HAVEN

Winter Haven went as smooth as silk except for one almost tragic accident. We were in the towing operation in the second contest day when, as a tow plane was taxing down the side of the runway toward the grid, the signal was given to launch the next sailplane. As towplane and sailplane approached the returning towplane, the sailplane dropped a wing (left wing down, looping to the right). The sailplane headed for the taxiing towplane, the two collided, with the right wing of the sailplane going into the prop. About one third of the wing was instantly chopped off. The prop made several cuts into the stub. The sailplane's right wing stub slid down the cowling of the L-19 towplane and smashed the wind screen. The wing strut of the towplane was hit so hard that it bent the wing down to about 30 degrees.

The sailplane was a Ventus. Both planes were severely damaged. Both pilots were OK with the tow pilot having a small scratch on his arm from the shattered plexiglass.

May 21, 1985

FUNNIES

I couldn't believe it but it was true. While in Winter Haven I had been doing my usual, sleeping on the airport at night, and like always I picked an out-of-the-way spot. About 2:30 am I am awakened by a big guy in a uniform asking me, "What time is the plane going to land?"

Now I didn't have my "jammies" on, and they won't let me grab anything in the van. But after I got out of the van they realized I didn't need to be searched. They asked for I.D. and I explained it was in my shorts. They let me put them on. I was informed that I was under suspicion of being a dope smuggler.

I tried to explain that I was with the sailplane race that was going on at the field. Then I made a worse mistake and tried to explain how sailplanes fly without engines. In the eyes of the law I was fast going from dope smuggler to being a "crazy."

After 15 minutes of confusion and the police checking with the airport manager, I was allowed to stay where I was. I should have realized that a van parked on a Florida airport at night back in the bushes is going to be checked out. <u>Bozo gets busted.</u>

Sailplane Racing News

June 27, 1986

PROFILE

Name: Garland Pack
Occupation: Flyer
Age: 73
Hometown: Murfreesboro, TN

I first met Garland in the early 1970's at the gliderport, Eagleville, Tennessee. He was one of those guys I take to pretty quick, because he always came to the point, and every delivery I made to Eagleville was paid in cash on the spot.

Garland taught himself to fly while in high school and took up barnstorming as soon as he could scrape up the dough to buy a J-3. He flew around the South giving rides for 50 cents or less if that's all you had. Garland got interested in air racing and built several midget racers and even won a few races. WW II came along and Garland joined up. He flew the Hump on more missions that he cared to remember. After the war he flew professionally and in the mid sixties started soaring.

He owned and ran Eagleville for some 25 years, using J-3's for tow planes with this own designed props, and TG-2's for training.

Garland introduced lots of folks to soaring, including several who are racing today.

Garland died March 28, 1986, from Parkinson's disease, a real loss to soaring. We'll miss you, Garland, you were our type of guy.

April 28, 1987

EDITORIAL

I'm writing this issue from the Open Class Nats in Minden. We have 25 entries. The weighing has been a real football ("I wish someone would let the air out."). The powers that be have finally come up with something to rival crewing for A.J. Smith. If you're the guy weighing sailplanes on the grid, "you only want to do it once." You cannot believe some of the things I've heard said.

Hope you can stabilize this problem. It's making a lot of folks mad and that's not what soaring is about. The weighing can be done but it's going to take a set procedure and cooperation from the pilots.

April 28, 1987

GOOD SPORTS, NO EXCUSES

I don't usually talk about the down side that some of the pilots have during a contest. But I'm mentioning it in this report because the answers I got when I asked "what happened?" gave me a real insight into why these guys are true champions. Doug Jacobs, on missing the last turn on the first day: "I just spaced it out." Klaus Holighaus on flying forty miles past the turn on the second day: "I ran out of brain!" Al Leffler on landing out the third day: "It was a combination of bad luck and stupidity, probably more the latter." Kees Musters: "I always hate it when it's my turn to lose."

No excuses, no whining, no "I'm going home." They told it like it was, and you knew it hurt. But they smiled and got right back in the game – true champions.

April 28, 1987

THE CODED START

With the go-ahead from the Competition Committee Chairman, we experimented with the "Coded Start." Pilots were given a folded paper with their code number inside. This was done just before launch on the grid. After the task was opened, the gate would accept three clicks on 123.3 as an indication of a plane on the I.P. The pilot made a normal run, and as he crossed the start line, he heard "Mark, Good Start" or "Bad Try" and then his code number.

Sailplane Racing News

The test was held under conditions of 4,000 feet or less altitude and 7/10 dark cloud cover. As long as the pilot received a good start he never had to speak over the radio. No one got a bad try and had to give the gate a verbal response (Maybe this is a new way to control start height.) The pressure was on the spotters to get the numbers, and they did it without a miss, proving once again that young eyes are the best. No one over the age of 15 was on the binocs. The test was a success and Eric Mozer has given the go-ahead to continue the experiment in regionals this summer. You will see a complete explanation in Sailplane Racing News soon.

May 17, 1989

NO MORNING PILOTS' MEETING

Another idea we tried at Chester, and it proved to be very popular, was eliminating the morning pilots meeting. We staged at 11a.m. with your plane off the side of the runway near your grid number. The pilots' meeting was called at the head of the grid 15 minutes later. The winners spoke, we covered the admin., had a weather briefing, handed out score and task sheets and announced grid time.

Normally, pilots had an hour to prepare their maps and eat lunch. This system also gave the organizers more time to print the handouts and the weatherman more time to collect data. No one complained. The organizer didn't have to find a place to hold the meeting and the pilots had plenty of uninterrupted time to prepare their ships. Chester plans to use this routine in the future.

May 17, 1989

WILDLIFE STORY

After a race day, John Murray pulled up to his tiedown and got out of the car, when suddenly he noticed a four-foot, totally harmless, rat snake (Southern term) coming toward him. John is afraid of snakes, no

See Ya' at the Airport

way around it. He has no use for the slithering creatures.

He immediately started shouting "Snake!" and doing a dance reminiscent of a punk rocker on steroids. The snake was unimpressed and continued on course towards the warm runway. John sees his neighbor's Volvo, leaps in and starts driving in circles trying to flatten the snake.

After a couple of close passes, the snake realizes this could be trouble and begins to seek a safe hiding place. The nearest he could find was the wheel well of John's AS-W 24. So with a quick slither the snake is now curled around the wheel and safe from the mad Volvo driver. By this time many of the folks in the tiedown area have heard the commotion and are moving toward the scene with drinks and folding chairs in hand to have a front-row seat for the show.

Johnny Byrd shows up and being an ole Everglades boy, says he'll get the snake out. Johnny suggests they turn the fuselage on its side, cycle the gear and see if the snake can be extracted. With Murray at the gear handle and Johnny at the gear doors, Murray cycles the gear. I know Murray had the snake's death in mind when he cycled the gear because it was done with great force. The snake made a desperate move to escape. This move also frightened Murray, who instantly cycled the gear again, trapping the snake in the gear doors.

Johnny Byrd moves quick and grabs the snake's head. The snake is trying to hold onto the gear. But with a great tug, Johnny has the snake in his hands and Murray is running in the opposite direction with eyes the size of silver dollars.

The snake was set free in the tree line behind the tiedowns and all returned to normal, until the next day when Murray was getting ready on the grid. He picked up his parachute out of the cockpit and two snakes were staring up at him. The reaction was almost as good as the day before, until John realized that both snakes were rubber and had green yaw strings taped to their heads. I wonder, isn't green Johnny Byrd's lucky color?

Sailplane Racing News

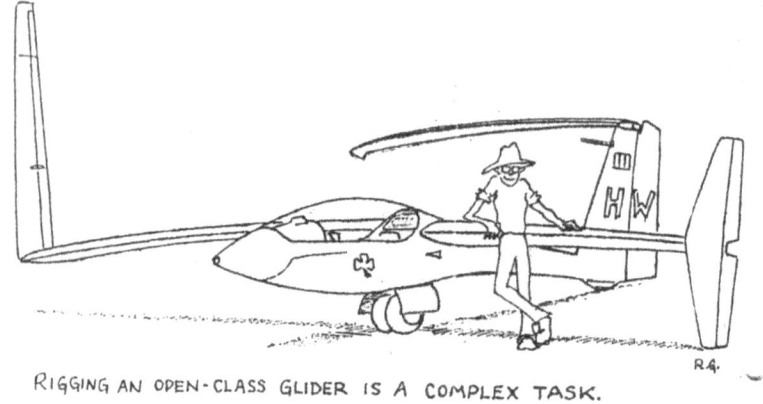

RIGGING AN OPEN-CLASS GLIDER IS A COMPLEX TASK.

August 31, 1989

SHOOTOUT AT UVALDE: 15 METER NATS

Hi Race Fans,

It's high noon on the hot dusty streets of Uvalde. Marshal Striedieck steps out into the street with a slow pace, looks in both directions and checks his "LS Six Shooter" slung low on his right hip, then adjusts his Stetson low over his eyes. The showdown is about to begin.

Down at the Tail Dolly Saloon the Dyson gang is hangin' out. Never was there a rougher, tougher bunch. The gang leader Dyson is gunning for his first kill. He's on edge, with an itchy trigger finger. Dyson's right-hand man is Pretty Face Mozer, a young gun with a reputation for shooting with no mercy. Johnny Byrd is standing at the bar mumbling to one of the showgirls. Johnny is a man of few words and lots of action, as dangerous as ever. Playing poker over in one corner is the California Kid, Ray Gimmey. The others at the table are String Bean Leffler, Shotgun Sorenson, Bad Bill Bartell and Roy "Killer" Cundiff, all ready for the shootout.

People scurry out of sight as the marshal walks slowly down the middle of Main Street. He stops and turns to face the swinging doors of the saloon. "All right, Dyson, you and your gang's time is up." A short pause hangs heavy, then the gang steps into the street and spreads out to face the marshal.

See Ya' at the Airport

"I gave you boys 'til noon to clear out. Now show your hand," the marshal says. Suddenly the air is filled with the sound and smoke of the shootout. As the air clears from the dust and the smell of cordite, Dyson is already mounting up and riding out of town, slightly wounded. Bad Bill Bartell is lying in the dust, dead from a well-aimed landout. The rest of the gang has been disarmed, and they've also mounted up and are heading into the sunset. Pretty Face Mozer has come the closest to the marshal but it didn't even make Striedieck flinch. He blows the smoke form the barrel of his gun, drops it in its holster and says, "We'll meet again, boys, in the badlands of Nevada."

We had fun at Uvalde. It was a clean, fair race, run safely without so much as a gear-up landing during the event. The weather was a mixed bag. Uvalde got its whole year's rainfall on the first contest day. Six inches fell in 12 hours. The next four days were weak but got progressively better as the ground dried out. We had the high thick cirrus from the monsoons in the Baja brought over Uvalde by a high-level high pressure system. It clamped the heat and cu's down and the vis was lowered. We stood down for a rest day on Monday and it was a good thing as a dry front came through the area. The soaring was the pits.

The last three days were Uvalde grade with streets hundreds of miles long, running down South as far as you could see into Old Mexico. Contest Day Seven was a true classic, a 294-mile call, Eagle Pass, Laredo, Farias and home. Striedieck won the Giltner trophy for the best speed on this day by doing the task at 88.31 mph.

See you at the airport.
Charlie.

Sailplane Racing News

February 3, 1988

CHARLIE'S PEOPLE

Sad news from Europe, Kees Musters was killed in a hang glider accident in France. Details are few, but it appears that Kees stalled on take off from a 150-meter-high cliff. Kees was a very popular international competitor. He won the 15m class at the 83 Hobbs internationals. Kees flew in both the Hitachi Masters of Soaring. He was a true champion and he will be missed.

October 6, 1989

SUBMARINE STORY

Tony Lauck had a real adventure at New Castle. After driving down from Boston, Tony arrived at the famous creek ford that leads to the New Castle gliderport. Rains had been heavy that afternoon and the creek was up. Tony drove down the dirt road that leads to the ford. Seeing the water up, he was apprehensive, but backing the car and trailer was all but impossible on the one-lane road in the rain. Tony decided to go for it.

With his crew, Chris, riding shotgun, Tony headed into the swollen creek in his new BMW. Things seemed to be OK but suddenly the trailer began to float and this turned the car upstream. Both Tony and Chris knew they were in big trouble when water began to come in around the doors. Within seconds the car was filled up to the seats with water, and shortly both driver and crew were chest deep in cold creek water. The engine took a gulp and died.

Tony and Chris now decide it's time to abandon ship. They open the door, which allows the creek to freeflow through the car. Both make shore safely.

Lanier Frantz comes to the rescue with the farm's largest tractor. After an hour the car and trailer are on dry land.

Tony, of course, is very upset and immediately begins to try to dry things out. In fact, when we packed up the contest, Tony was still working on the car. It ran once for a few minutes on Tuesday but hasn't hit a lick since.

Of course the jokes and jibes were coming hot and heavy. Like: Is that a fuzzbuster on the dash of Tony's car? No, it's a fishfinder....Tony, what time are you planning to set sail for home? ...We understand Tony's having the horn replaced with submarine dive claxtons. ...and many, many more. Tony took all the joking in stride and says he hopes they name the bridge after him if they ever build it. Tough luck.

October 16, 1989

FUNNIES

Working on the gate at Uvalde, one of the ladies was discussing the fact that her husband had retired in January. How's it going? we all asked. She replied that it hadn't worked out so well, "I ended up with twice as much husband and half as much money!"

CHARLIE'S PEOPLE

September 6, 1988
Michelle Sorenson is pregnant. But it's even greater news that after some tests, the doctors have determined that she will have twin boys! Nothing like doubling the size of your family in one fell swoop.

September 7, 1990
Evelyn Pakosta was crewing Fred at Littlefield when she stepped into an armadillo hole and twisted her knee so bad she had to spend the night in the hospital. She insisted Fred fly the next day, and the good crew that she is, she worked 123.5 from her hospital room!

May 20, 1994
Bob Fitch passed away this Easter. After a day of soaring at his

home airport of Blairstown, Bob went home, lay down and it was over. Bob was a true supporter of soaring. Not only did he fly in many contests, all over the East Coast, but he was a member of our world team, crewing Doug Jacobs when he won the championship in Rieti.

Bob was never on top of the score sheet, but he was at the top of his game when it came to people. I can remember many night sitting around the camping area of Elmira, Dansville, Fairfield, and Chester with Bob and the gang. Bob truly enjoyed this part of soaring the best, and was always in the thick of any conversation. He was one of the best "liars dice" players I've ever seen, and his taste in jokes was right down my alley.

Bob took his obligation to soaring seriously by being on the SSA Board of Directors for two terms, and was very active in his local club. When the sailplanes are put away for the day, the beer is coming out of the cooler, the jokes are racy, and the dice can be heard shaking in the can, you will be sorely missed, Bob.

The French have really developed team flying and they used it very well in the World Championships. So much so that they inspired this cartoon in the daily program.

See Ya' at the Airport

August 3, 1990

SOARING FUN IN ODESSA: 1-26 CHAMPIONSHIP

Hi Race Fans,

Forty 1-26ers showed up in Odessa, Texas, to fly the 26th Annual 1-26 Championships. Fun is the main thing with these pilots and they had plenty of it on this first contest day as all the contestants got back to Eagle Field after flying a 130-mile task. Gary Evans did this task at a speed of 54 mph, pretty spiffy for a 30-year-old-design sailplane.

The flying fun went into the tank on the following day, as a very rare Canadian cold front pushed all the way down to the Texas-Mexico border. The daily temperatures went from 100 degrees to the low 70s and the lift was non-existent. We lost five of the scheduled eight days to this front as it stalled and backed up, then charged over us, again and again.

The last two days were POST days, due mainly to the weak lift. The POST gave the pilots a chance to make it a contest by being able to go where they wanted. Dave Mockler won his fourth 1-26 title by a slim 22-point decision over John Cravance.

The contest was flown off the Eagle Nest gliderport run by Juan Batch. This is a great soaring site – large runways, big hangars, plenty of friendly folks. If you get a chance, check this operation out. Sailplanes are their only traffic. To prove this is a great site, on the first of July Wally Scott flew his AS-W 20 out of Eagle Nest to land in Nebraska 729 miles away.

There were a couple of interesting retrieves during this contest. The first was Irn Jousma's. Irnie landed about five miles from the home drome in a "buffalo waller." Irn's wife Karen got the message and took out in the direction of the "waller." She was soon lost, and after standing on top of the van, she called on 123.5 to say she couldn't find her pilot.

Tow pilot Hurricane Duwane Moore took off and flew over the landout, giving Karen directions. The directions were pretty mundane: turn right, follow the ruts, take the left fork. Then came the direction that caught everyone's ear: "OK, keep coming, when you get to the dead cow, turn right. Your pilot is over the next rise." Sure enough,

Karen found the dead cow and with her two boys leaning out the window to make sure the cow was really dead, she found her pilot.

The next interesting retrieve was done by Dan Mockler and his wife Silvia. Dan landed on the main road about six miles from the airport. Now, Dan is a fierce competitor and he knew the day was dying and he was behind. So with a little help from a couple of retired naval admirals, Dan tied a 40-foot rope to the back of his trailer and began to fly behind it down the highway, with the admirals giving marks for every overhead wire and every roadside sign.

The road had a sharp turn in it and Dan realized he couldn't make the turn. He released, pulled up, cut the corner and again landed on the highway. He hooked up again and started out for the airport. Here is where the reports get foggy. Some claim that the 18-wheeler came to a screeching halt as Dan released and headed for the runway. Others say the truck was not that close but it did slow down quickly.

Many who heard the story the first time laughed and said Dan showed some good ole-time gumption. But after thinking twice, all realized this was dangerous and could have made us very high profile. The competition committee decided that a 100-point penalty should demonstrate that this was not the thing to do.

The 1-26 Association is growing, 20 percent over the last three years. The amount of care given to these birds is very obvious. There are some really stunning paint jobs on many of the ships, and many are covering their metal wings with fabric for better surfaces.

Next year the 1-26ers will be in Ohio at Caesar Creek, looking for that soaring fun.

See you at the airport.
Charlie

See Ya' at the Airport

October 19, 1990

SUPER TASK: NEW CASTLE

It was a long wait, but it was worth it. After 10 years of hoping, watching and planning, the perfect day finally arrived. As contestants showed up for the 1990 Region 6 South Championships, the talk was already focused on Monday. It looked as if the classic type of front was forming and moving toward the Appalachian ridges.

On practice day, several pilots declared and flew 500k tasks. Starting out good!! The first race day was a speed triangle flown on thermals. With the big front approaching this task was a slight overcall at 118 miles and 50 percent of the fleet made it around the track. Best speed was 60 mph.

With the computer humming and printing the DUAT program, spitting out weather maps and progs, it became obvious that Contest Day Two was exactly what we had waited for all these years, the 1000k task.

A pilots' meeting was called in the White House. All the pilots gathered around the large relief map of the ridges from Pennsylvania down to Georgia.

The Bedford, Penn., turnpoint had been in the turnpoint book from the beginning but never used. Now all eyes were on this turnpoint and the terrain between it and home, New Castle.

The task was laid out, down to the tunnel, up to Bedford, down to the quarry and back to New Castle. There was real excitement in the air during this meeting. Veteran ridge runners discussed every phase of the task from the rocket ridge to the tunnel to the dreaded Knoblies – the softest part of the trip, where to land all along the route, the procedures for passing each other on the ridge. After two hours on intense pilot meeting, the grid time was set for 8 a.m. the next morning.

As the sun rose in a clear sky, pilots and crews readied the ships for the long task. Loaded them with ballast, sandwiches and fruit in the side pocket, sectionals with task marked, folded and stowed, all were ready as the sniffer launched down the dew-covered grass runway.

Sailplane Racing News

Soon the word came – "The ridge is working."

We all hold our breath as the heavy sailplanes launch one by one. In 40 minutes, all are airborne and the 1000k task is opened at 9:10 a.m. Within 15 minutes the gate is quiet and all are on task.

The first hour or so is weak, and the advisors are in the lead making safety calls for those who follow. As high noon arrives, the ridge is stronger and thermals are present. It looks as if things are really go.

The day is a "keeper" and in a little more than 7 ½ hours, 16 pilots have completed 626.8 miles, the longest task yet called in an American soaring contest. The fastest pilot was John Seymour at 86 mph. The slowest was Kai Gertsen at 64 mph (Kai flew without ballast due to dump valve problems.)

Six of the pilots declared for their 1000k diploma. New Castle is so remote that all turns are photographed according to FAI rules.

This was a great experience for everyone involved. The tension of the start, the excitement of the pilots who flew it, and the exhilaration of the completion made for a wonderful soaring event, long to be remembered by all who were there.

The front that created this day also clamped the soaring down for two days afterwards, and it looked for a while that the 1000k would not be part of an official contest. Thursday was an over cast day with several layers of clouds above us. The air was humid and it seemed dead. We gridded with a small hope that the coming new front would arrive early and give us northwest winds.

At 1 p.m. the sniffer launched. The ridge lift was just enough to give him an 80-knot ride. The task was Big Walker Tunnel and back, a distance of 128 miles. All who launched made the task and assured that New Castle had a contest with three official days.

New Castle is a unique soaring site. It's got a charm that cannot be found anywhere else. Add to that the thrill of a 1000k flight, a couple of great social events including Ed Kilbourne's performing his new Cloudbase concert, and a lot of very interesting pilots and crews, and you've got racing at its best.

See you at the airport.
Charlie.

See Ya' at the Airport

June 20, 1991

LINCOLN AWARD

Sailplane Racing News has been given a great honor. I and the newsletter have been awarded the Lincoln Award for writing that promotes the sport of soaring. This award means a great deal to me. Never in my wildest thoughts did I think I could win this prestigious acknowledgement for my writing. I must give Janice Hoke a lot of the credit for being the best editor I could have. She cleans me up without whitewashing, and she is the mechanic that gets the newsletter assembled. Thanks to the Harris Hill Corp. for this honor. I plan to live up to its charter.

June 20, 1991

PROFILE

Name: Rick Walters
Age: 36
Occupation: Contractor
Hometown: Minden

Rick is a big fellow at 6 ft. 6 in and 240 pounds which makes fitting him in a sailplane somewhat of a problem. He's a real problem to those he competes against, too. This guy is tough and getting tougher.

Rick got interested in soaring through model flying. He was the Western Champion in RC sailplanes and was a member of the World RC sailplane team.

Rick has taken the summer off, packed up his pickup truck and Discus, and is flying every National. He's the most enthusiastic racer I've seen in a while, working hard to get all the lessons he can in this sport. He has the talent and he's getting the education. You will hear from this guy; he's planning to blow your doors off.

Sailplane Racing News

August 23, 1991

EDITORIAL

I don't know whether to laugh, cry, pray, or cuss over our move to the 35mm film system. Probably laugh, and also cuss for all the guys who lost heavily this season due to camera and film problems.

I am beginning to really appreciate those 1-26 cameras and that film loading system more and more at each contest. It would be great to return to the system that was almost foolproof, when we went for contest after contest without a point lost to camera problems.

Today, that is no longer the way it is. I have seen four complete camera failures this season. All four resulted in great loss of points through no fault of the pilot. Walt Cawby lost the Manning regional to a double camera failure, Sam Giltner lost both films at Hobbs, George Moffat lost both cameras to film problems at the Opens in Marfa, and one of the Italians in Uvalde went from seventh place to the bottom of the score sheet due to camera failure, and there were countless others who had one camera go down on any given contest day.

I never dreamed there could be as many different ways for these cameras to fail as I have seen over the past two years, I am afraid we are victims of "wand waving," that old magician's trick where things are not as perceived. I have seen organizers buy every kind of cheap film they can lay their hands on, trying to save some of the money that goes into the contest. (The second largest cost at a contest is the film.)

I've seen film so thick and strong that the Army could use it for tank treads, and it did a great job of tearing out the little plastic teeth that move the film through the camera. I've seen hand-rolled film that was so tight in the camera that only a few cameras manufactured by the Hercules company could get it to go through. I've seen film that for no reason would suddenly be rewound by the camera.

* * *

So the pilot is left with that ole favorite game played by all Florida tourists with their cameras – "What do I set this thing at?" This game has resulted in film with nothing on it, to film that looks as if someone stuck a welding torch through the lens. I've watched two competitors smash their cameras on the tarmac this year, something I haven't seen since the days of A.J. Smith.

As entertaining as all this is, it indicates we do not have a real grip on the problem of proof. No pilot who has taken the time and money to race deserves to be hammered by the system. Saving a few bucks cannot make up for a 4,000-mile drive with a sailplane in tow and all the other expenses it takes to race, all to be screwed by a $1.25 piece of film.

The problem is simple – we have been put in the film wilderness, and we must find a way out quick. (....) Let's all get busy and start to solve this problem by getting the contest committee to select one type of film for next season. No matter what it is, at least we'll know what to do with it after a couple of races.

December, 1992

WHAT'S HOT

What is the hottest item in racing? Cellular phones. This year in the Nationals several pilots were carrying them in the cockpit. The guys rented system time in Reno or Lubbock, and at both sites the phone came in very handy after landouts. Now if GPS comes into racing and is combined with the phones, a pilot could call in his location within seconds of his landing. Sounds very safe to me: however, would we allow pilot-to-pilot calls, and can the pilot call back to the crew at the motel during a flight?

December 8, 1995

EAGLE FIELD UPDATE

Karl Striedieck reports that although there have been delays in the schedule for building a new highway over Bald Eagle Ridge, the project is still alive and bulldozers may begin in 1998. Following a letter-writing campaign two years ago, PennDOT received over 250 letters from concerned individuals in the US and numerous foreign countries including Zimbabwe, Lithuania, Finland, Switzerland and New Zealand among others. The environmental impact document noted this wide-spread interest from the international glider community and also took note of correspondence from falconers, bird-watchers, bird clubs, fire tower fans and the SSA's historic glider site committee.

Although it is likely that around 40 acres may be taken for this road, consulting engineering firms have indicated that measures can be taken to limit the impact on flying. Karl thanks the hundreds of individuals who cared enough to write and offers each author a free Jeep tow.

April 4, 1996

AN ERA COMES TO AN END

For the first time in 26 years there will not be a contest at Chester. A combination of things brought an era to an end. The Chester Soaring Club has shrunk over the past few years with members not reupping and new members not materializing. The TCA at Charlotte has grown to the point that we had to make a special effort each year to keep several of our turnpoints open to us. With opening of a commercial operation in Spartanburg, S.C., some of our members began getting tows from there. Last year's contest drew about 30 pilots, not quite enough to break even.

I am truly sad about this turn of events. I have been at all 26 contests. Chester is the place I first fell in love with racing. I will miss the first race of the season when new ships and new pilots were put to the test for the first time. Joe Giltner was the guy who put it together for the first time way back in 1969, and the racers this race drew are unparalleled anywhere else in racing. Greene, Beltz, Moffat, Mozer, Striedieck, Byrd, Gimmey, Johnson, Butler, Smith and Jacobs are some of the names that have been on the scoresheets of Chester.

Dogwoods in bloom, azaleas in full color, and the smell of

honeysuckle marked the start of Chester. The sound of peeper frogs at dusk, and the haunting call of the whippoorwills marked the start of Chester. Most of all the friends who drive in from all over with a smile on their faces that shakes the chill of winter and brings the warm breezes we all crave marked the start of Chester.

Gren Seibels still holds the record for the number of consecutive years as Chester's organizer. He and Trudy were mainstays of this contest. I can still hear Gren's voice in those all-important pilots meetings, and I can still hear his wonderful stories as the sunset to the tinkle of mixed drinks.

Joe Giltner was everywhere doing everything to make this contest go like greased lightning. In 1978, there were 78 ships on the grid, and I remember that Joe launched them all in 56 minutes. I remember the sight we saw when we returned to the airport after a tornado ripped through it.

Names like Lew McDonald, Dickie Blackburn, Scott Mayes, Dick Fuller, Fred McFawn, Sam Lyons, Sam Crane, and so many others are fading even as I write. It was these people who came time and time again to make the race run right and enjoy being a part of it.

Sam Giltner made an effort to breathe life back into the Chester race, but without the club and support from others it was a futile endeavor. One last attempt was mounted by Joe Ownsby but he too ran into the same problems.

I hope that we can revive this Championship soon. When April rolls around, I will be even sadder than now. I know there will be others who will feel the same. I hope that in the very near future we will again see silent white wings crossing the finish line at Chester, and know that it will be that way long into the future.

September 3, 1993

CHARLIE'S PEOPLE

Sad news: Art Haseltine passed away this spring. Art was crew for Bobby Bridges at many races. Art really liked racing and was a frequent visitor to the international meets. Art had not been around lately, but he kept up with the news through this newsletter.

Art was a positive guy. I can remember a rained-out task at Cordele on the banquet day. Art came into the golf club where the banquet was being held as he was leaving on retrieve. We all got a good laugh as he poured two iced teas, put plates and silverware on the table, and as he walked out he said, "We'll be right back." The retrieve was some 60 miles away.

Once, Bobby was leading a race until he landed out on the second-to-last day. Bobby was standing in the retrieve office, filling out his card, and giving us a sob story. When he finished, Art looked over at him and said, "Well, buddy, you had 'em fooled for a little while." Bobby broke into a laugh, and Art said, "Let's eat, I'm buying." Art was a good SCUM.

See Ya' at the Airport

June 28, 1996

FUNNIES

Definitions:

Wiley POST – Head off into unknown territory, with no assurance of return.

Emily POST – Politely tiptoe around the three closest turnpoints.

Saturday Evening POST – Wait until the last possible moment to head out on task, then scramble to get back home before dark.

Scratching POST – Fly at the lowest possible altitude.

Parcel POST – Head out into the wild blue, never to be heard of again.

Washington POST – Have unnamed source reveal the task before the pilots' meeting.

Army POST – All contestants run the task in close formation, in order of contest number.

Hitchin' POST – Tag along with yesterday's winner.

Dumb as a POST – Stay in the start gate until the CD gets irate.

POST mortem – Fly the task, then argue about it all night long.

SIDEBAR

During the late 80's, there was a spirited discussion going on in the contest community as to whether Charlie was qualified to be the CD at a National Contest. Two of the letters that appeared on this topic in Soaring Magazine, are re-published here. Charlie CD' ed his first National Contest in 1990.

Consideration for Charlie Spratt
Published in 'Soaring Mail', Soaring Magazine, May 1990

In the last few years, I have been greatly encouraged to see a solution emerging for our Competition Director shortage. Charlie Spratt has been CDing regional contests and now has more than 30 under his belt, which means he probably has more CD experience than anyone else in the US. He has the same shortcoming (no recent racing experience) as most of the recent US national and international contest CD's. However, he still has as good or better qualifications as about any CD in recent years.

Sidebar

To gauge his reputation and respect among US racing pilots, and to reveal or banish any reservations about Spratt's qualifications, we posed a question on the 1989 Sailplane Racing Association annual poll about his suitability. The results were that an overwhelming 90.4% of the respondents agreed that Charlie was qualified to be CD at a National contest.

Charlie has been approached on several occasions the last two years about being a CD for a Nationals. The SSA Contest Board has indicated that Charlie would not be allowed to do so.

Board Chairman Linke indicated to me that he discussed this matter with most of the SSA Directors and found a "significant" number had "serious reservations" about Charlie as Nationals CD. In light of this feedback, he felt it best to decline permission at this time. Linke is not closing the door on the future and will be anxious to hear how Charlie does at CDing the National Sports/Motorglider Nationals at Littlefield this season. Linke also mentioned the not surprising fact that Charlie's major supporters (but not all) are in the East and his major detractors (but not all) are in the West.

My observations and discussions with many SSA Directors and dozens of racing pilots leads me to conclude that most Directors and a vast majority (90.4%) of racing pilots are pro-Charlie and his detractors are a few powerful Directors of the SSA power structure.

Those of us who recognize the great contribution to soaring racing made by Charlie are profoundly disappointed in the Contest Boards decision. We feel this major resource is being jeopardized.

What do I mean by jeopardized? I mean I stay fearful that Charlie may become discouraged and turn his back on our sport. Remember, his kicks come on the ground, not in the air like us. And, it's not like we pay him so much that he can't afford to quit. If we adopt camera starts, abolish the gate and refuse to let him be CD then we can't blame him for becoming discouraged.

If you share my opinions about Charlie, then raise a hue and cry with your SSA Director

ED BYARS
Clemson, SC

See Ya' at the Airport

Kudos for Charlie
Published in 'Soaring Mail', Soaring Magazine, October 1992

A year or two ago there was considerable correspondence in the "Soaring Mail" column — sometimes pretty acerbic — over the fitness of Charlie Spratt to be a contest director on the Nationals level. Despite Charlie's vast experience and involvement in sailplane racing for twenty years, some felt that this lack of experience as a pilot would be an overriding detriment.

This year I have flown in two contests CD'd by Charlie, the Open Nationals and the Masters in Florida. Both were characterized by difficult, iffy weather, and in both Charlie did as fine a job as I have seen in contest career embracing upwards of 30 National and World contests in seven countries.

What makes Charlie so good? There are many factors. High on the list is an unusual combination of willingness to listen coupled with decisiveness. In all too many CD's of my experience, including some very famous ones, one has to make do with one but not both of the qualities, leading to indecision on the one hand or an arbitrary I'm-right-so-don't-bother-me attitude on the other.

An example of Charlie's ability came on the last day of the Opens when all pilots launched, and it became clear that none of the four assigned task options would yield a fair contest. It took less than five minutes for Charlie to consult with his two pilot advisors on 123.3, ask scorer Jim Bobo to punch up two alternative possibilities, select one and send the pilots out into the only soarable quadrant available. Common sense? Sure but it isn't so common. How many times have we all flown impossible tasks because the CD felt he couldn't modify an early call?

What else makes Charlie so good? He cares. He really cares. There is a visible empathy between Charlie and the pilots, unlike the them/us attitude that is all too frequent. Another factor is the sheer number of contests that Charlie directs; three Nationals this year and a countless backlog of Regionals in the past. Most Nationals level CD's direct every three to five years and the rust often shows. It's a demanding job — like instrument flying — and it takes recent experience, lots of it, to stay sharp.

Sidebar

I've flown under some excellent CD's — Darrel Watson comes to mind among the recent ones. In my experience, Charlie Spratt is right up there at the top of the list, only fitting for someone who has given so much to sailplane racing. It's hard to imagine our sport without his distinctive contributions. No Sailplane Racing News? No marvelously expressive idioms, okay, it's elephant walk time, that's a real worm burner. No crystal clear "Good start X-ray, X-ray!" We would be the less, very much the less without him.

And as a Nationals CD? "Good start, great start, Charlie Sierra!"

GEORGE B. MOFFAT
Marion, MA

ACKNOWLEDGMENTS

This book came about with the help of many people. What started out as a collaboration between Charlie Spratt, John Good and me on behalf of the National Soaring Museum, grew into a project that involved many members of the soaring community. In addition to thanking all who offered their encouragement throughout the year and a half it took to complete this book, here are those we'd like to thank by name:

First and foremost, John Good for his work as editor. After years of working with Charlie, John knew how to walk a fine line, editing Charlie's stories yet preserving Charlie's unique storyteller's voice.

Chris Woods for helping with the selection of photographs that we collected from many sources: the National Soaring Museum's archives with the help of NSM curator Bill Gallagher, Charlie's own collection of family photographs, Brian & Sherry Milner, Sam & Leigh Zimmerman, Karl & Iris Striedieck, Lee Kuhlke and Chris Woods. The photographs used on the cover are from Chris Woods, Brian & Sherry Milner and Charlie.

The drawings found throughout the book are by Greg Rosplock, a Harris Hill Soaring Corp. junior member. With a few strokes of a pen, he was able to artfully capture the essence of the story.

Acknowledgments

Kirby Best, glider pilot and president of Lightning Source, for acting as our printer and for all his encouragement and patience in answering my ignorant questions.

Bernie Paiewonsky, NSM trustee and Chair of the NSM publications committee, for his valued input at the early stages of this project.

Anne Touvell, Assistant to the NSM director, for creating the manuscript. With her computer skills, creativity and efficiency, she took a load off my shoulders and was a key person to this project.

The cover was created by another member of the soaring family; Andrea Weissenbuehler. Thank you for giving this book such a 'fresh' face!

Many thanks also to Karl Striedieck, George Moffat and NSM Director Peter W. Smith for their accolades printed on the back of the cover and their support throughout the project.

In the fall of 2003 the National Soaring Museum organized a fundraiser to help defray the cost of this first NSM publication. We'd like to thank all who so generously contributed and hope you like what we created. We hope this will be the first of many books about soaring and about, as Charlie puts it so eloquently, the glue that holds us all together.

And finally, thank you Charlie for writing these colorful stories that paint such a clear and dear picture of contest soaring life, and that make us laugh.

Karin A. Schlösser
NSM Trustee

www.ingramcontent.com/pod-product-compliance
Lightning Source LLC
Chambersburg PA
CBHW032044150426
43194CB00006B/418